50 One-Minute Tips for Better Communication

Speak, write and present more effectively

Third Edition

Phillip E. Bozek, Ph. D.

A Crisp Fifty-Minute™ Series Book

AXZO PRESS

50 One-Minute Tips for Better Communication

Speak, write and present more effectively

Third Edition

Phillip E. Bozek, Ph. D.

CREDITS:

President, Axzo Press:	**Jon Winder**
Vice President, Product Development:	**Charles G. Blum**
Vice President, Operations:	**Josh Pincus**
Director, Publishing Systems Development:	**Dan Quackenbush**
Developmental Editor:	**Jim O'Shea**
Copy Editor:	**Catherine E. Oliver**

ISBN 10: 1-4260-1840-1
ISBN 13: 978-1-4260-1840-4

Printed in the United States of America

2 3 4 5 6 7 8 9 10   13 12 11 10

Table of Contents

About the Author

Phillip Bozek is the president of Communication Designs Inc., a training company located in Tampa, Florida. Communication Designs delivers training programs and coaching sessions in presentation skills, interactive training skills, e-mail and document writing, technical writing, meeting management, facilitation skills, and coaching skills.

Dr. Bozek's clients have included 3M, Alcon Laboratories, AmeriNet, Barrick Gold, General Motors, MasterCard, L-3 Communications, Los Alamos National Laboratory, Nextel, Prudential, Rio Tinto, the United States Army, the United States Postal Service, and Volkswagen.

Dr. Bozek can be reached on the Web at www.communicationdesignsinc.com or by phone at 1-727-423-4324.

Preface

Leading and attending meetings, writing business documents, and giving presentations are some of the most important communication activities in business. As a business professional, you can greatly enhance your own and your organization's success by improving your skills in these areas.

▶ **Meetings.** Millions of business meetings are held every day in organizations around the globe. Because flatter management hierarchies and team decision-making have become commonplace, effective meetings are more important than ever. As you rise in your organization, you are almost certain to attend more meetings, so your skills as a meeting leader or participant can be keys to your success.

This book offers several strategies for improving the quality of your in-person meetings, and it includes a special set of strategies for improving teleconferences.

▶ **E-mail and documents.** Documenting your ideas and accomplishments is critical to your organization's progress and to your personal record of contributions. Moreover, a large part of many professionals' average day consists of reading business documents, so the best business writers make their documents as easy as possible to read.

This book offers techniques that will help you write more easily and make your writing more reader friendly.

▶ **Presentations.** Studies have shown that skill in presenting is one of the most accurate predictors of professional success. This means that some of the most important moments in your career will occur when you stand up to present ideas to colleagues. Your listeners will associate the quality of your presentation technique with the quality of your thinking and with your very identity as a professional. Excellent technique will not only help you achieve your goals but also enhance your professional credibility and self-esteem.

This book proposes several techniques that can help you create and deliver clear, well-organized, appropriately enthusiastic business presentations.

▶ **PowerPoint.** Using PowerPoint well can greatly enhance your effectiveness as a presenter; using it poorly can cause "Death by PowerPoint."

This book's fourth section suggests some innovative ways to prepare and deliver PowerPoint slideshows. I have included only techniques that I have found especially helpful for my own presentations. I hope these techniques also help you create highly organized slideshows that complement your physical presentation and give your listeners a clear, coherent message.

▶ **Exercises.** This book contains many references to electronic versions of the forms, exercises, and files discussed in the text. I invite you to download these resources at www.axzopress.com and use them to produce excellent meetings, documents, presentations, and PowerPoint slideshows.

My goal is to give you ideas to help your business communications become more clear and productive, and in doing so, help your business relationships become more harmonious and satisfying.

Phillip E. Bozek, President
Communication Designs, Inc.

Learning Objectives

Complete this book, and you'll know how to:

1) Conduct productive meetings

2) Implement effective business writing methods

3) Create and give efficient and successful business presentations

4) Take advantage of Microsoft PowerPoint as you prepare and deliver presentations

Workplace and Management Competencies mapping

For over 30 years, business and industry has utilized competency models to select employees. The trend to use competency-based approaches in education and training, assessment, and development of workers has experienced a more recent emergence within the Employment and Training Administration (ETA), a division of the United States Department of Labor.

The ETA's General Competency Model Framework spans a wide array of competencies from the more basic competencies, such as reading and writing, to more advanced occupation-specific competencies. The Crisp Series finds its home in what the ETA refers to as the Workplace Competencies and the Management Competencies.

50 One-Minute Tips for Better Communication covers information vital to mastering the following competencies:

Workplace Competencies:

▶ Customer Focus

▶ Working with Tools & Technology

Management Competencies:

▶ Informing

▶ Clarifying Roles & Objectives

For a comprehensive mapping of Crisp Series titles to the Workplace and Management competencies, visit www.CrispSeries.com.

About the Crisp 50-Minute Series

The Crisp 50-Minute Series was designed to cover critical business and professional development topics in the shortest possible time. Our easy-to-read, easy-to-understand format can be used for self-study or for classroom training. With a wealth of hands-on exercises, the 50-Minute books keep you engaged and help you retain critical skills.

What You Need to Know

We designed the Crisp 50-Minute Series to be as self-explanatory as possible. But there are a few things you should know before you begin the book.

Exercises

Exercises look like this:

EXERCISE TITLE

Questions and other information would be here.

Keep a pencil handy. Any time you see an exercise, you should try to complete it. If the exercise has specific answers, an answer key will be provided in the appendix. (Some exercises ask you to think about your own opinions or situation; these types of exercises will not have answer keys.)

Forms

A heading like this means that the rest of the page is a form:

FORMHEAD

Forms are meant to be reusable. You might want to make a photocopy of a form before you fill it out, so that you can use it again later.

A Note to Instructors

We've tried to make the Crisp 50-Minute Series books as useful as possible as classroom training manuals. Here are some of the features we provide for instructors:

- ▶ PowerPoint presentations
- ▶ Answer keys
- ▶ Assessments
- ▶ Customization

PowerPoint Presentations

You can download a PowerPoint presentation for this book from our Web site at www.CrispSeries.com.

Answer keys

If an exercise has specific answers, an answer key will be provided in the appendix. (Some exercises ask you to think about your own opinions or situation; these types of exercises will not have answer keys.)

Assessments

For each 50-Minute Series book, we have developed a 35- to 50-item assessment. The assessment for this book is available at www.CrispSeries.com. *Assessments should not be used in any employee-selection process.*

Customization

Crisp books can be quickly and easily customized to meet your needs—from adding your logo to developing proprietary content. Crisp books are available in print and electronic form. For more information on customization, see www.CrispSeries.com.

Fourteen Tips to Improve Your Meetings

Fourteen Tips to Improve Your Meetings

The first section of this book is designed to help you make your business meetings better by using, among other things, facilitation skills. But the term *facilitation skills* applies to three different skill sets: *pure facilitation*, a set of group-process skills delivered by a neutral outsider; *training facilitation*, a set of interactive techniques used by teachers; and *facilitative team leadership*, a set of skills for team leaders who run participatory, discussion-oriented meetings. This book focuses on facilitative team leadership.

How good are your facilitative team leadership skills now? The "How Do You Meet?" survey will help you find out. This survey is available for downloading from www.axzopress.com.

When you're planning your next meeting, ask yourself:

- ▶ Is this meeting really necessary? Tip 1 will help you decide.

- ▶ If you need to set up a business meeting, Tips 2 and 3 will help you do so successfully.

OK, your meeting is ready to go. Now how do you begin it? See Tip 4. How do you lead a meeting effectively? See Tips 5–9.

How do you close meetings effectively and evaluate them so you can improve future meetings? See Tips 10 and 11.

For ideas on making informal meetings, one-on-one meetings, and teleconferences more effective, see Tips 11–14.

For a form that summarizes basic planning for meetings in general—a "Bonus" Tip, if you will—see the Meeting Planning Guide at the end of this chapter.

If you would like more information on the general topic of meetings and facilitation, and on some of the specific Tips in this book, please see these other Axzo Press publications:

- ▶ *Achieving Consensus* by Jon Scott and Eileen Flanigan. Eileen and I collaborated on a version of the "How Do You Meet?" survey.

- ▶ *Effective Meeting Skills,* by Marion Hayes, provides more information on Tips 2 and 3.

- ▶ *Facilitation Skills for Team Leaders,* by Donald Hackett and Charles L. Martin, provides more information on Tips 2, 3, and 9.

Tip 1: Think of Meetings as Investments

Suppose you think your office could use a new high-speed copy machine—a significant expense. In your company, you wouldn't need to get any approvals or even consider the matter carefully—you'd just run right out and buy one, right? Wrong. You would need to think before you spent that kind of money.

But when it comes to spending money on meetings, people often don't think first. Some organizations call meetings on a moment's notice and drag them on for hours, tying up valuable time and resources—often with no thought about how expensive meetings really are. And meetings can be *very* expensive investments. Consider:

▶ **Salaries** — Each person at that meeting draws a salary for his or her attendance.

▶ **Benefits** — Each person at the meeting receives benefits. Benefit packages can average about 33% of salary.

▶ **Opportunity costs** — The people in your meeting have probably been called away from their principal duties. Studies estimate that professionals typically attend about 60 meetings per month, and that as much as 50% of the time spent in most meetings is wasted. So if the typical meeting averages one hour, that equals four days of time wasted per month. As Peter Drucker once said, "One either meets or one works—one cannot do both at the same time." This means that unless your meetings are really good ones, lots of time and productivity are being lost.

Aside from these costs, think about other meeting-cost factors: the expense of the room, rental or depreciation on electronic equipment, refreshment costs, and so on. Also, consider how poorly run or unnecessary meetings can damage morale. Harold Reimer, a meeting productivity consultant, once estimated that the average company loses $800 per year per employee on the "meeting recovery syndrome"—the time people spend around the water cooler complaining about bad meetings.

To determine how much a typical meeting in your organization costs, and whether you are paying more for your meetings than you thought, do the exercise that starts on the next page. This exercise is also available as a download on the Axzo Press Web site.

Think Purposes, Not Necessarily Meetings

If you find that your meetings are too expensive, ask yourself if you really need all those meetings to get things done. Maybe you don't. A way to find out is to think purposes, not meetings. Before you resort to another meeting, identify what you want to accomplish and consider what other forms of communication might accomplish your purposes. Download the exercise called "To Meet—or Not to Meet?" from the Axzo Press Web site.

ARE YOU PAYING FINES FOR YOUR COMPANY MEETINGS?

Does your organization pay "meeting fines"—hidden financial penalties for poorly run meetings? To find out, think of one typical meeting you've attended recently—maybe one that didn't seem very productive—grab a calculator, and fill out the form below:

1. Length of the meeting (in hours).   _____

2. Number of people at the meeting.   _____

3. **Person-hour investment.** Multiply line 1 by line 2.   _____

4. Estimated yearly salary of an average participant. $_____

5. **Average hourly salary.** Divide line 4 by 2,000. $_____

6. Add **benefits per hour.** Multiply line 5 by 4/3. $_____

7. Add **opportunity cost** (revenue participants would have generated on the job). Double line 6. $_____

8. **Total person-cost per hour.** Multiply line 7 by line 2. $_____

9. **Total meeting person-cost.** Multiply line 8 by line 1. $_____

10. Of the people at the meeting, how many were critical to the purpose of the meeting?   _____

11. **Personnel efficiency.** Divide line 10 by line 2.   _____

12. How long (in hours) should the meeting really have taken to accomplish its purposes? (Consider whether the meeting started late, got off track, and so on.)   _____

13. **Time efficiency.** Divide line 12 by line 1.   _____

14. **Total meeting efficiency.** Multiply line 11 by line 13.   _____

15. **Total return on meeting investment.** Multiply line 9 by line 14. $_____

16. **Your meeting fine.** Subtract line 15 from line 9. $_____

Line 16 represents the money your organization loses on every typical meeting. How much do you lose yearly? Multiply line 16 by the number of meetings your organization holds per year.

The figure you get may surprise you. As you can see, meetings can be very expensive. If you're spending more than you want to on meetings, keep reading this book!

Tip 2: Forecast Your Meetings

Maybe you've heard a meeting start out with this sentence: "I suppose you're all wondering why I've called this meeting…." If you have heard this, chances are that the meeting that ensued was not as productive as it could have been. Why not? Meeting participants weren't prepared.

Unless you, as a meeting leader, have a specific, good reason for doing otherwise, give meeting participants at least the following information beforehand:

▶ The purpose of the meeting

▶ The agenda or outline

▶ The outcomes expected from the meeting

▶ The meeting's start and end times

You might also want to inform the participants:

▶ What kinds of information will be expected from them

▶ What they should do to prepare for the meeting

▶ When they can expect breaks, if the meeting is long

If the meeting will have a written agenda, forecasting is easy—just send out the agenda early. Even if the meeting is a quickly convened ad hoc gathering, give participants a brief forecast of the meeting when you invite them. (For more on ad hoc meetings, see Tip 12.)

If You're a Participant, Ask!

Every person at a meeting should feel responsible for the meeting's success. When you're invited to a meeting whose purpose is unclear, ask—find out what you can bring that will help the meeting work better. Remember, it's your time and your meeting, too. Make your meetings successful—know the forecast, and be prepared when you walk in.

Try This Agenda/Minutes Form

Have a look at the example of an Agenda/Minutes form on the next page. This form is used by a Fortune 500 firm that has efficient, well-run meetings. An electronic version of this form is available for you on the Axzo Press Web site.

Green Belt Project – Improve Quality of New Hires Weekly Team Minutes

Date	Time & Location	Attendees	
Feb 18th	9:30am – 10:30am, Boardroom **Passcode:** 775 0000	D. Fufufnik N. Animal Y. Knot	R. Eddy B. Karloff A. Simpson
Next meeting: Feb 25th	10:00am – 12:00pm, Boardroom		

Agenda
- Define project charter
- Establish tentative project close timeframe
- Establish future meeting dates and times

Topics/ Objectives	Key Points / Decisions	Action Items	Status

Define Project Charter	• Need to define what is meant by "quality new hire":
	  o EC&DP ratings may be too subjective
	  o Results of SMARTS Objectives may provide data points
	  o May require supervisor interviews/surveys
	• This project could affect the counter balance of D's time to hire Green Belt Project
	• The project scope may be too big
	  o Sales hires may be a good starting place
	  o We will ask J to help us focus on an appropriate project scope
		TEAM: Check with J. Burke during 2/25 meeting
		
		D. Fufufnik: Finalize charter by 3/1
		
		B. Karloff: Arrange for J to help us with scope, by 2/20	

Establish project close timeframe	• A. Simpson suggested a 4-5 month timeframe • After today's discussion, the team feels a minimum of 5-6 months is an appropriate timeframe	**R. Eddy:** Clear timeframe recommendation with J. Crenshaw by 3/1	John approved a 7/31 close date
Establish future meeting dates and times	• Team opted to meet weekly for two hours • Tuesdays, 10am – 12pm as a rule of thumb	**Y. Knot:** Set up meeting schedule by 2/22. Every other Tuesday, 10-11am	Meetings set up in Lotus Notes

Items For Next Meeting/Parking Lot
- Clarify project charter issues and scope with Black Belt
- Establish tentative milestones
- Clarify how AP prefers to work with our team

Sample meeting agenda with minutes

Tip 3: Use "Meeting Focus" Posters in Meeting Rooms

Companies that have productive meetings often use professionally prepared "meeting focus" wall posters in their meeting rooms. As part of your meeting room décor, try using some permanent posters as well as some flipcharts.

Permanent Posters

Here are two permanent posters typical of the ones I have seen hanging in the meeting rooms of companies with especially good meetings:

Before Meetings, Ask Yourself:	**Our Ground Rules For Meetings:**
• Do you know this meeting's purpose? • Do you have an agenda? • What is your role? • Are you willing to take action?	• Be prepared • Be on time • Stay on track • No side conversations • Phones on "vibrate" • Everyone participates • All ideas have value

Note that ground rules for meetings might not work very well if they are composed by the meeting leader working alone. Ground rules will work better if the team "owns" them, so teams should brainstorm their own rules and at least post them on a flipchart. Save the flipchart and make it into a nice poster if you can, but in any case, have the rules available for the team to see at every subsequent meeting.

Temporary Flipcharts

Public category minutes. Have you ever wondered what that minute-taker in the back of the room is recording, or worried that something vital will be missed? Worse yet, have you ever dreaded the idea that *you* might have to take the minutes?

If so, try using public category minutes. Select the categories of information that you'll need; label separate flipchart pages with the categories; then record the contributions to each category on the flipcharts, right in front of everyone.

Using public category minutes gives your team several benefits:

▶ **Conciseness and completeness** — You record only what's essential.

▶ **Accuracy** — Everyone sees what's recorded and can fix mistakes immediately.

▶ **Focus** — Discussions stay on track, without endless recycling, because everyone can see where discussions have already been.

▶ **Improved understanding** — Agreements, disagreements, and complex issues are more easily clarified if they're conveyed visually as well as verbally.

▶ **Quick publication** — When the meeting is finished, simply have the flipcharts typed up and e-mailed.

When using public category minutes:

1. Consider the categories of "Key Decisions" and "Action Items." These may be all you need. However, match the categories to your meeting's purposes.

2. Encourage note-takers to record the exact words of participants. Abbreviating is OK, but paraphrasing might not be.

3. Take turns being the note-taker, maybe even during the course of one meeting.

The "Parking Lot." Another useful visual to have in a meeting room is a "Parking Lot" flipchart for capturing ideas not relevant to the meeting's agenda, but worth discussing later. Parking lots can help you keep meetings focused on the agenda without restricting the free flow of ideas.

When using a parking lot, make sure the team decides when the parking lot ideas will be processed, and make sure the team processes them as planned. If a parking lot becomes a "garbage can," it won't work very well!

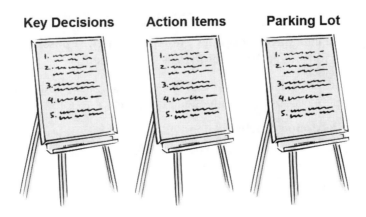

Key Decisions   **Action Items**   **Parking Lot**

Tip 4: Use a "Recipe" to Start Meetings Well

Preparation is the key to managing any meeting-leadership jitters you may experience. If you prepare what you're going to do and say to open your meetings, your stress will decrease, and you'll get the meeting off to a productive start.

Experiment with this recipe to organize the openings of your meetings.

A Meeting Opening Recipe

1. **Begin on time.**

2. **Welcome everyone.** Say hello in a strong, confident voice. If the group is new, let people introduce themselves. If the group has met before, make sure to introduce any guests or new members.

3. **Summarize the meeting's purpose.** Describe the intended outcomes of the meeting. Use "team" language, not "boss" language (not "What I want to accomplish" but rather, "What we want to accomplish"). Be brief.

4. **Review the agenda.** Of course, you have distributed the agenda beforehand and have brought spares for people who forgot their copies. Have a "public" copy of the agenda on a slide or flipchart for all to see—it will help keep the group focused throughout the meeting.

5. **If appropriate, review the minutes and the evaluation (see Tip 11) of the last meeting.**

6. **Set, suggest, or review ground rules for the meeting.** Ask participants, "Do we all agree to these?" Get a "yes" from every person—don't assume silence means agreement.

7. **If appropriate, distribute and explain new materials.**

8. **Clarify the role of the recorder and timekeeper.** If possible, get volunteers for these jobs rather than assigning them.

9. **Solicit questions.** Ask if everyone is clear about what you've proposed for the meeting's process. Again, get each participant to agree.

10. **Initiate discussion** of agenda item 1.

Tip 5: Know How Effective Leaders Behave

Remember Michael Scott, the manager played by actor Steve Carell on the TV show *The Office?* Was Michael a true and powerful leader of the Dunder Mifflin Paper Supply Company?

What do you mean, "No, not really"? He had the title, didn't he? He had the suit and the sign on the door, didn't he? "Yes," you reply, "but he didn't have his team's respect." You're absolutely right—a title doesn't make a leader. Real leadership is earned, not given.

True leaders earn leadership, whether of an empire or a staff meeting. How does a person earn leadership status? By the way she or he acts in the group. In his book *Small Group Decisionmaking*, B. Aubrey Fisher describes the typical behaviors exhibited by individuals who emerge as the natural leaders of otherwise leaderless group discussions. Listed below are some notes on key behaviors to help you identify ways to gain, maintain, or build your leadership in your organization's meetings.

Listed below are some notes on key behaviors to help you identify ways to gain, maintain, or build your leadership in your organization's meetings:

1. **Ask questions early.** Early in the discussion, natural leaders tend to solicit the views of other group members.

2. **Make frequent, short contributions to the discussion.** Leaders interject frequent comments, but not necessarily lengthy ones. Leaders make quick suggestions for directing or changing the flow of the discussion—but their comments don't dominate the overall talk time of the group. (See Tip 6.)

3. **Give informed, objective views.** Leaders do their homework on the issues. When they do give their views, they are well-informed views, expressed with conviction. From the views of others, leaders can impartially identify those ideas that are most valuable.

4. **Exhibit dynamic nonverbal communication.** Natural leaders tend to have steady eye contact, strong and highly inflected voices (i.e., with lots of intonation; see Tip 36), dynamic gestures and body movements, and expressive facial animation.

Tip 6: 10 Key Statements of Effective Meeting Leaders

Natural meeting leaders contribute frequent short comments to direct the flow of meeting discussions. Here's a list of specific phrases such leaders might use. Listen for these or similar phrases at your next meeting; the people offering them are probably doing a lot to help (that is, lead) the group.

Here are statements you might hear from leaders directing discussions at meetings:

1. **"Let's try (X)…" or "Should we try (X)?"** A suggestion that the group try a new approach, either to a problem or to the discussion of a problem.

2. **"What are your thoughts?"** A request for input, directed to one or more participants.

3. **"So what you're saying is…"** An attempt to reflect or clarify what has just been said, and perhaps to relate it to a previous comment.

4. **"OK, thanks."** Natural leaders acknowledge team members and their contributions, without necessarily evaluating the contributions as good or bad.

5. **"Are we getting off track?"** To control digressions, the leader is asking for the group's help rather than ordering the digression to stop.

6. **"Let's remember our ground rules."** An attempt to encourage diplomacy or protect a group member from a harsh statement by another.

7. **"Your turn, then yours."** Natural leaders help maintain order in enthusiastic discussions by making sure everyone gets heard.

8. **"Can we all live with that?"** This is the all-important consensus question. Make sure you get a reaction from each participant before you proceed. If some don't agree, talk it out. Without buy-in, you won't know if your meeting's progress is real. Remember that a good meeting is a series of small agreements.

9. **"What have we decided?"** Summarizing periodically during the meeting, as well as at the meeting's end, is critical to a productive meeting.

10. **"Who is going to do what by when?"** If no specific action is taken as a result of the meeting, was the meeting really worthwhile?

And another key "statement" is *silence*, a surprisingly important responsibility of a good meeting leader. Monitor your own talk time, and make fair time available to all meeting participants. Especially if you supervise the participants, don't dominate team discussions. Let team members give their ideas before you give yours.

To practice these meeting leaders' key statements and question-asking skills, see the Axzo Press Web site and download the exercises named "Improving Not-So-Great Statements of Meeting Leaders" and "Using Questions to Manage Discussions."

Tip 7: Use "Funneling" to Brainstorm on Single Issues

"Funneling" is a group technique we can borrow from the world of training facilitation. Trainers need to get a lot of information exchanged clearly and quickly—which is also the goal of any business meeting. So, in your meetings, try funneling—you will find a hundred uses for this very flexible brainstorming tool. (If you're a trainer, you may recognize funneling as a streamlined version of the "nominal group technique.") Here's how you conduct funneling exercises:

Funneling

PURPOSE: To identify and prioritize lists of needs, concerns, opinions, or observations of participants about one issue

DURATION: 20–35 minutes

MATERIALS NEEDED: Flipchart pages or whiteboard; marking pens; pens and paper for participants

1. **Preliminaries.** Decide what issue you want the group to discuss. Tell participants that they will be participating in a small group brainstorming activity to generate a list of concerns or observations on the issue.

2. **Team formation.** Divide the participants into teams of two to seven people (three to five works best). Ask each team to appoint one member as the brainstorm note-taker.

3. **Idea generation.** Ask all teams to brainstorm as many ideas as they can on the issue in a specified number of minutes (four to seven minutes works well, depending on the complexity of the issue). Encourage teams to work quickly, without evaluating ideas. The team note-taker records all ideas on one or two sheets of paper.

4. **Prioritization of team data.** Ask all teams to discuss and quickly come to a consensus on the three or four best ideas from the list they have generated. Allow them only one or two minutes.

5. **Presentation of results.** Announce that the flipchart represents the group's top priorities on the issue in question.

Tip 8: Use "Fast Networks" to Brainstorm on Multiple Issues

The "Fast Networks" technique is another way to energize your meetings—to get things done and have some fun. Fast Networks is a training facilitation technique that lends itself to brainstorming and "group concern" meetings that address multiple issues. The technique involves lots of walking around and lots of organized creativity; it works best for groups of eight or more people.

Fast Networks[*]

PURPOSE: To identify needs, concerns, opinions, or observations of meeting participants about several issues

DURATION: 20–35 minutes

MATERIALS NEEDED: Flipchart pages or multiple whiteboards; marking pens; pens and paper for participants.

1. **Preliminaries.** Decide what kind of information you want to get from the group—opinions, ideas, attitudes, or the like. Plan to have as many teams as you have categories of information—for example, if you want the group's opinions about four issues, divide participants into four teams.

2. **Team formation.** Divide the participants into as many teams as there are categories of information (try to have two to seven people on each team; three to five is best). Tell teams they will be responsible for gathering information on their topic from the *entire group*—not just their own team members, but everybody on all the other teams as well—and that they must work quickly.

3. **(Optional) Planning session.** Give each team one or two minutes to devise a strategy for collecting the assigned information from the entire group.

4. **Idea collection.** Begin the data collection period. Allow 5–10 minutes.

5. **Summarizing data.** Recall the teams and ask each team to retire to a corner, process the data, and produce a summary report on a flipchart. Give them 5–10 minutes to prepare. Encourage the teams to work quickly.

6. **Presenting results.** Announce the start of the "Show and Tell" period. Give each team a short time (about a minute and a half) to present results.

7. **(Optional) Evaluation and award ceremony.** Ask each participant to write down a vote for the best all-around presentation. Tally and announce the results. Award a prize of some kind.

[*] "Fast Networks" is based on concepts articulated by Sivasailam Thiagarajan in *Games, Etc.: How to Improve Learning, Performance, and Productivity.*

Tip 9: Use the FAST Formula to Manage "Meeting Theft"

"Meeting thefts" are behaviors that steal time, productivity, or good will from business meetings. Behaviors that "steal" include talking too much, criticizing too quickly, carrying on side conversations, telling too many jokes or digressive stories, or arriving late or unprepared. Because such behaviors devalue meetings, they are genuine forms of business thievery.

Yet the culprits themselves deserve to be treated with kindness and diplomacy, for an important reason—many meeting thieves are well-intentioned people who may be unaware that their behaviors are counterproductive.

A Solution: Use FAST Diplomacy

This talking technique can coach a thief into more productive action:

Face the problem;

Acknowledge the person and his or her good intentions;

Suggest a new behavior;

Try again, perhaps by modifying or escalating your approach.

For example, suppose a team member is always telling jokes. Let's call him Hugh Morownly. Hugh is funny, but he's throwing the meeting off track. To manage him:

Face: Look right at him and say, "Excuse me, Hugh, let me make a suggestion…"

Acknowledge: "First, your jokes are great…"

Suggest: "…and yet I still don't know what that good mind of yours really thinks about this issue. Seriously, can you tell us what you recommend?"

Try again: If he persists, perhaps you get a bit tougher: "Hey Hugh, come on. We've had some good fun, but what's the bottom line here?"

If these public interventions still don't work, ask Hugh if you can talk to him on a break. In private, tell him what you see him doing, how you interpret his actions, how you feel about them, and what you want him to do. Be assertive and more firm than you were in public.

For a practice exercise, download "The FAST Technique" from the Axzo Press Web site.

Additional Ideas for Managing Meeting Theft

1. Remember to refer to the team's ground rules.

2. Manage all "thefts" without inflicting public embarrassment. Handle serious issues in private, off-line conversations.

3. Remember, meeting leaders are not the only ones who manage theft. Every person at the meeting should be responsible to keep him- or herself and other participants on track. A good way to help each other is to agree upon a signal—like a referee's time-out, with hands forming a T—that any participant can use to flag an off-track digression or other problem. Another signal everyone can use is a device like a TWIDLR.

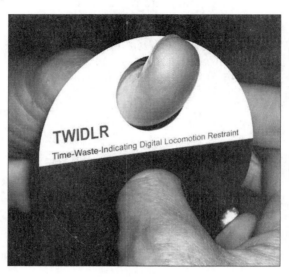

The TWIDLR

How to Use a TWIDLR

The TWIDLR—i.e., "Time-Waste Indicating Digital Locomotion Restraint"—looks like a toy, and it is. But it works! I'm told NASA has used something like it at staff meetings, and found that they reduced the length of meetings by over 25%.

Here's how it works: Anyone who thinks the meeting is going awry just spins a TWIDLR on his or her fingers, sending a subtle signal that the team is getting off track. When the meeting "thieves" see the signal, it might be just enough of a gentle reminder to fix the problem.

How to Get TWIDLRS

You can contact me at www.communicationdesignsinc.com, tell me how many you need, and I'll arrange to send them to you.

Tip 10: Use a "Recipe" to Finish Meetings Well

The end of a meeting is critical. Lots of issues might still be open: Did we get anything decided? Who will do what now? Did we finish what we needed to? How did the meeting go? When and where is the next one? What can we do better at the next meeting? Are there any final thoughts to share now? Will this meeting end on a positive note? Do we have energy at the end, or just exhaustion and frustration?

To address these issues, experiment with this recipe to organize the meeting's closing.

A Meeting Conclusion Recipe

1. **Announce that the end of the meeting is at hand.**

2. **Summarize key decisions and action items** and other key results of the meeting. This will be easy if you have been using public category minutes (see Tip 3). Ensure that everyone knows who is doing what action item by when.

3. **Review the agenda.** Indicate what was covered and what might still need to be covered; identify possible agenda items for the next meeting.

4. **Set up the next meeting.** Agree on the next meeting's date, time, and location.

5. **Arrange for the distribution of minutes.** This will be easy if you have been using public category minutes—you just take the flipcharts, type them up, and send them out.

6. **Consider giving every participant a "last word."** Invite any participant who wishes to make a final, very brief closing comment to do so.

7. **Evaluate the meeting.** See Tip 11 for some interesting ways to do this.

8. **Close on a positive note.** Congratulate participants on their performance, express your appreciation, and close with a big "Thank you!"

Tip 11: Evaluate Meetings to Ensure Productivity

Things left uninspected begin to deteriorate."

–Dwight D. Eisenhower

Meetings are a big part of most organizations' activities and therefore a big responsibility for many professionals. But oddly, few organizations systematically evaluate their meetings, even though these organizations might be meticulous about evaluating other aspects of performance.

To ensure that your group's meetings are as productive as they can be, and to avoid the deterioration that President Eisenhower's quote predicts, evaluate your meetings.

You won't need feedback on every single meeting, especially if your group meets regularly. Evaluating every third or fourth meeting will be sufficient to monitor quality.

You might want to use an open-ended format like the one provided here, or the more specific "Meeting Evaluation Form," available on the Axzo Press Web site.

Meeting Evaluation

TO:
FROM:
DATE:
SUBJECT: Evaluation of Meeting

Date of meeting:
Title/Subject of meeting:

1. What was good about the meeting:

2. Suggestions for the next meeting:

Tip 12: Quick Strategies for Ad Hoc Meetings

Many businesses have informal or ad hoc meetings, called quickly and conducted without a written agenda. Although such meetings are impossible to plan in detail, many things can be done to ensure that they run efficiently:

▶ **Consider your purposes** before you call a meeting. Are you sure you need a meeting? Will an e-mail message, a text message, or a few phone calls achieve your purpose just as well?

▶ **Tell participants what the meeting is about** and what they should do before the meeting. If you're a participant, ask.

▶ **Clarify the start and end times** of the meeting.

▶ **Limit the agenda.** You're much better off making some progress on a few topics than no progress on many.

▶ **Start on time.**

▶ **Announce the agenda** at the meeting's start. Write the agenda on a flipchart or a whiteboard.

▶ **Rein in digressions.**

▶ **Speak concisely** and encourage others to do so also.

▶ **Establish an open, supportive atmosphere.**

▶ **Stay vigilant about the agenda and the time.** Remind your colleagues (and yourself) to stay on topic and on time.

▶ **If the meeting is long, give breaks.** Try frequent, short, precisely timed breaks, rather than long, less frequent, or vaguely timed breaks.

▶ **Summarize** the progress of the meeting periodically.

▶ **Clarify key decisions and action items** at the end of the meeting. Specify who has agreed to do what by when.

▶ **End on time**—or a little before.

Tip 13: Quick Strategies for One-on-One Meetings

▶ **Request and plan for regular one-on-one meetings with your boss.** Although ad hoc meetings are useful, don't depend on them for all of the vital exchanges that are the lifeblood of business. Instead, let regularly scheduled one-on-one meetings replace some of the ad hoc meetings you have with your boss. You might both get more done.

▶ **Schedule it short and keep it short.** Fifteen or so minutes every week might be all you need—if you're organized before and during the meeting.

▶ **Make it "your" meeting.** Get your boss to agree that this meeting is for your agenda. His or her issues are important, but agree to save them for team meetings, or at least for another meeting. Make this meeting yours.

▶ **Follow a prioritized agenda.** Have it ready and waiting. Discuss the most important items first. Don't try to cover too much—better some progress on few issues than no progress on many.

▶ **Bring solutions, not just problems.** Bring clear descriptions of problems and issues you're facing, but also bring your best solution, your best alternatives for solutions, or at least your criteria for what a good solution should do. In short, help your boss answer your questions.

▶ **Speak concisely.** Think "sound bites." Give the overview, not the details—unless they are absolutely essential or your boss requests them. Remember, the boss manages the big picture, not the details.

▶ **Listen hard.** Good listening is the key to communication.

▶ **Summarize at the end of the meeting.** Reconfirm what decisions you and your boss have made and who is supposed to do what. Record key decisions and action plans.

▶ **Encourage your subordinates to schedule "their" meetings with you.** Let them set their own agendas, just as you set yours with your superior. At "their" meetings, listen more than you talk.

Tip 14: Use Special Strategies for Teleconferences

Before the Teleconference

▶ Keep the number of participants as small as possible. Communication difficulties grow quickly as the number of participants increases.

▶ When scheduling meeting times, be aware of time-zone differences. Consider lunch hours, optimum times of day, rush hours, and so on.

▶ To avoid distracting external noise, reserve a soundproof conference room. If possible, use a room that will not have a noisy meeting taking place next door.

▶ Distribute to every location the meeting announcement or agenda and any other materials. Be sure to number agenda items, and formulate them as objectives to reach. Add an estimated time frame for each agenda item.

▶ Make sure participants know the date and time of the conference call. Send a reminder and ask for a confirmation from each participant.

At the Start of the Teleconference

▶ Facilitate introductions of all parties on the call. Participants should introduce themselves so that they can be identified by their voices.

▶ If needed, remind participants of any agreed-upon ground rules regarding speaking up, eliminating side conversations, checking for understanding, and avoiding interruptions.

▶ Arrange for someone other than the meeting leader/facilitator to take minutes, and designate someone else to keep track of time.

During the Teleconference

▶ Be aware that teleconference (and videoconference and Web conference) communication is more difficult because body-language cues are missing, incomplete, or hard to see.

▶ Encourage people to identify themselves before they speak.

▶ Encourage everyone to speak slowly, clearly, and simply. If appropriate, remind everyone that dialect and accent challenges are enhanced during conference calls. Avoid jargon and acronyms that might not be clear to everyone, and define any you use.

▶ Because voice-activated microphones can cut off a speaker if others speak before she or he is done, be sure the speaker is finished before you begin.

▶ Eliminate side conversations; they can cut off a speaker. Use the mute button if side talk or side noises are necessary.

▶ Do not take silence as agreement. Be careful about checking for understanding, especially with less vocal meeting participants.

▶ To avoid having everyone talk at once, direct questions and comments to specific individuals or locations.

▶ If someone arrives late, wait for a pause and say, "Everyone, we have a newcomer. Please introduce yourself briefly." Then say "Great, thanks, [Name]. Now, where were we?"

▶ Take minutes about key decisions and action items.

▶ Use verbal techniques to facilitate the group and overcome the limits of teleconferencing:

1. To avoid your first word being cut off, preface key ideas with:

"My view is that…"

"I think that…"

"The way to do this is…"

"Well…"

2. To signal the end of your point and relinquish your turn, summarize by saying:

"And so…"

"So my point is…"

3. To check if you've been heard and understood, add a tag question such as:

"Have I said that clearly?"

"Do you see what I'm saying?"

"How was that?"

4. To check your own understanding of a point or to emphasize another's point, say:

"So your idea is…"

"So what you're saying is…"

5. To speak after being silent for a while, say your name: "This is Doreen…."

6. Use others' names frequently, especially if you are directing a comment to someone specific or someone in the room with you.

7. To disagree diplomatically, preface your statements with "softeners" like:

   "I guess what I don't understand is…"

   "What I need more clarification on is…"

   "Here's another perspective…"

8. To move out of a tangled discussion, interject a high-level suggestion or question such as:

   "So what's the bottom line?"

   "All right, so where do we go from here?"

   "So how do we tie all this to our objective?"

9. To move to the next agenda item, summarize with, "So are we all OK on item 4?" Then introduce the next item by number and name.

At the End of the Teleconference

▶ Clarify key decisions and action items.

▶ Ask if there are any other open issues, and identify how they will be addressed (next meeting, separate meeting, online, offline, and so on).

▶ Briefly set up the next meeting, if necessary, and plan to publish the date, time, and location of the next meeting at the top of the minutes you send out.

A Final Word about Remote Meetings

Don't expect the same results from teleconferences, videoconferences, and Web conferences as you would expect from face-to-face meetings. People might be inhibited by the technology, so they might feel somewhat disconnected. Remote meetings work better when the people involved know each other from previous live meetings.

Ask remote team members to let you know whenever they plan to be on site, and take any opportunity to bring the team together face to face. This will greatly enhance their ability to communicate remotely.

A Meeting Planning Guide

1. **Know the meeting's purposes**

   General purposes   *Specific outcomes desired*

2. **Consider alternatives to holding a meeting**

   Will any other medium achieve the purposes and outcomes in specified in #1?

   ❑ Phone/V-mail   ❑ E-mail   ❑ Text/I.M.   ❑ Memo

   ❑ One-on-One   ❑ Newsletter   ❑ Bulletin Board   ❑ Other: _____

3. **Know the meeting participants**

   Name   *Why invite? What is his/her role?*
   Name   *Why invite? What is his/her role?*

4. **Notes on meeting date/time**

5. **Notes on meeting location**

   Room/building:
   Equipment/facilities needed:

   ❑

   ❑

   ❑

6. **Prepare agenda**

   (See Tip 2 and the online Meeting Announcement, Agenda, and Minutes form)

7. **Perform other tasks**

   ❑   Send the announcement/agenda to everyone

   ❑   Check on participants with assignments

   ❑   Confirm attendance of key participants

   ❑

   ❑

Note: This Meeting Planning Guide is available for you to download from the Axzo Press Web site.

Fourteen Tips to Improve Your Business Writing

Fourteen Tips To Improve Your Business Writing

You can rate your present writing practices by filling out the "How Do You Write?" survey, available for downloading from the Axzo Press Web site.

Tip 15 explains some common myths that inhibit some writers' ability to write effectively. Tip 16 shows how to plan a writing project to make it flow more easily.

Once you've planned a writing project, the next step is to get creative. Tip 17 guides you through several techniques for brainstorming ideas. Tip 18 will help you organize your e-mail messages and documents so your message gets across, even if your reader only scans your text quickly.

Now comes the challenge: Putting pen to paper (i.e., fingers to keyboard). See Tip 19 for ideas on how to use "Aerobic Writing" to write quickly and well.

The last step in producing good writing is revising. Tips 20–25 offer you tools for shaping what you've written into a concise, easy-to-read e-mail message or document.

Tip 26 gives you some suggestions for e-mail format and etiquette, and Tips 27–28 offer some special suggestions for technical writers.

At the end of this chapter, you'll find the outline for a writing process that will help you become more systematic when writing substantial business documents. It's the A-POWR process: Analyze, Produce, Organize, Write, Revise.

Note: Axzo Press offers many fine books on the subject of business writing (see the Axzo Press Web site). If you would like more information related to some of this book's specific Tips, see the works below:

- ▶ For more on Tips 17 and 23, see *Better Business Writing* by Susan Brock.

- ▶ For more on Tip 23, see *Writing Fitness* by Jack Swenson.

- ▶ For more on Tip 26, see *E-Mail Management* by Nancy Flynn.

Tip 15: Know the Facts and Myths About Business Writing

The sentences below are some of the attitudes, opinions, and comments about business writing I have heard and collected over the years. I often ask the business professionals in my writing workshops if they think these statements are generally accurate enough to call "facts" or inaccurate enough to call "myths." Let's see how you do with these.

BUSINESS WRITING: FACT OR MYTH

Please read each sentence below and mark it as either a fact (F) or a myth (M).

_____ 1. Readers read every e-mail message or document they receive.

_____ 2. Readers choose which e-mail messages to open by checking subject lines and senders.

_____ 3. Readers usually want as much information as they can get.

_____ 4. Writers usually save time by trying to write perfectly the first time.

_____ 5. In writing, big words are better because they're more professional.

_____ 6. Most readers would rather have three or four short e-mail messages on separate subjects than one long e-mail message on three or four subjects.

_____ 7. Editing and revising are critical when you write most business documents.

_____ 8. Any given e-mail message should be sent to everyone who might be interested.

_____ 9. Readers are generally the same; they read everything carefully.

_____ 10. When writing, using words like "I," "you," and "we" is unprofessional.

_____ 11. Always try to put everything you're writing onto one page.

_____ 12. It's OK to copy another writer's format.

Compare your responses to the author's answer key in the Appendix.

Tip 16: Ask Yourself Questions Before You Give Answers

Abraham Lincoln once said, "When I'm getting ready to reason with a man, I spend one-third of the time thinking about myself—what I'm going to say—and two-thirds thinking about him and what he's going to say." A similar process should become part of good business writing. Spend time thinking about what you plan to say, and spend even more time thinking about the people to whom you're going to say it.

Planning Saves Time and Effort

Planning before you write will make the writing task less difficult. Planning also saves you time—some of the decisions you write down in your planning process may become word-for-word renditions of key statements in your final memo.

Use the Planning Forms

The next exercise, called "Analyzing Reader Personalities," can help business writers adapt to the personalities and preferences of their readers. This exercise is also available for you to download from the Axzo Press Web site.

Also on the Axzo Press Web site is a Document Planner Form, listing several key planning issues to consider before you write business or technical documents. For shorter documents, you might need to think about only a few of these issues. For longer, more complex, or more important documents, you might need to address all of the issues and perhaps even add a few of your own. You can also use the "Analyzing Reader Personalities" form to clarify writing assignments from your supervisors.

Please feel free to duplicate or adapt these forms to use for planning your future documents.

Plan Your Writing in Writing

Plan your documents in writing, not just in your head. If you write your plans down, you'll not only remember them more clearly—you'll also be less likely to get confused when you're doing several projects at the same time.

ANALYZING READER PERSONALITIES

Make several copies of this blank form.

Give a copy of this form to any person whose "reading personality" you'd like to know more about—e.g., someone for whom you are writing a document, someone you write to frequently, or someone you'll be working with on a project. If the person would also like to know about your reading personality, give him or her a second copy of the form.

Keep one or two blank copies of the form yourself. On one copy, fill in the other person's name and mark what you think his or her reading preferences are. If he or she is guessing about you, too, take another form and fill in your own name and preferences.

Then exchange forms and talk about how good your guesses were. Have fun!

Form completed by: _____

When you write to (name) _____, he/she likes:

1. A formal tone	Yes	No	Depends
2. An informal, friendly tone	Yes	No	Depends
3. Emphasis on getting to the point, conciseness	Yes	No	Depends
4. Lots of examples/data/supporting material	Yes	No	Depends
5. Emphasis on reason and logical structure	Yes	No	Depends
6. Emphasis on creative speculation	Yes	No	Depends
7. A traditional professional vocabulary	Yes	No	Depends
8. Emoticons, like :) or :(	Yes	No	Depends
9. Abbreviations like LOL, NLT, COB	Yes	No	Depends
10. Emphasis on results	Yes	No	Depends
11. Emphasis on accuracy	Yes	No	Depends
12. Emphasis on teamwork and harmony	Yes	No	Depends

CONTINUED

CONTINUED

13.	Emphasis on policy and procedure	Yes	No	Depends
14.	Emphasis on open exchange of new ideas	Yes	No	Depends
15.	Short simple sentences	Yes	No	Depends
16.	Bullet points	Yes	No	Depends
17.	Highlighting (boldface, underlining, etc.)	Yes	No	Depends
18.	"Skim/scan/skip" reading	Yes	No	Depends
19.	Full sequential reading	Yes	No	Depends

Tip 17: Brainstorm Now, Organize Later

Suppose your team is tossing ideas around about the next company picnic. Jenny says, "How about a South Sea Islands theme?" Brian immediately says, "That's a stupid idea." What happens to Jenny? She becomes very quiet—no more ideas from her. Brian's comment cuts Jenny out of the process and will probably inhibit others' contributions, too.

Premature Criticism Kills the Creative Process

Few of us would be that cruel to another person. And yet we may be that cruel to ourselves when we write. When writing, do you ever think of an idea, type it, and then immediately delete it? Or worry if it's appropriate? Worse, do you ever just stare into space, not writing at all until you have the "perfect" idea?

Premature self-criticism is one of the chief causes of writer's block and of a general dislike for writing. It's also a costly waste of time.

The Brainstorming Attitude

The solution to premature criticism is to take a different approach: brainstorming, the rapid creation of lots of unedited ideas. Brainstorming postpones perfection to gain high-output creativity. Brainstorming is sometimes mistrusted and neglected, especially by technical people who are trained to do things right the first time. In writing, however, a perfectionist attitude can waste time. When you're brainstorming, you need to let go and have fun. Brainstorm it now; perfect it later.

Brainstorming Guidelines

When doing any brainstorming—composing a report, designing a presentation, or participating in group brainstorming at a meeting—keep these guidelines in mind:

- ▶ Think energy! Write as fast as you can!
- ▶ Record as many ideas as possible. Write everything down.
- ▶ Ignore spelling, punctuation, and sentence structure. Use abbreviations.
- ▶ Accept every idea, even weird ones. For now, it's all good!
- ▶ Start anywhere and feel free to jump around among ideas.
- ▶ Write until you burn out; rest; repeat!

The rest of this Tip suggests three ways to apply brainstorming in your business writing.

1. "Cluster" Brainstorming

A good technique to brainstorm a brand-new topic is to make "cluster" diagrams of your ideas. Clustering looks like the diagram below—a diagram I used to brainstorm this page. (Look carefully; you'll see virtually all of the page's ideas.)

Clustering lets you work with words in a nonlinear, almost pictorial way; you create both design and language, using both the right and left sides of your brain. Clustering is quick, and it's fun. Clustering is also interruptible; because it's nonlinear, you can easily stop now and continue later.

How to Use Cluster Brainstorming

Write your topic in a circle in the middle of a blank page (in our example, the word "clustering"). Radiate spokes and circles out from this center as you think of subtopics or ideas that connect to the main topic. Label these new circles however you want—perhaps with the names of sections of your memo, or perhaps with a journalist's standard questions (who, what, where, why, when, how), which I used in my example. (In my cluster I also added a circle called "Action Requests," which is a useful category to include in many business documents.)

When you cluster, work quickly. Skip around all you want. Don't worry about perfection, neatness, or even where you record a given idea. In other words, use a brainstorming attitude!

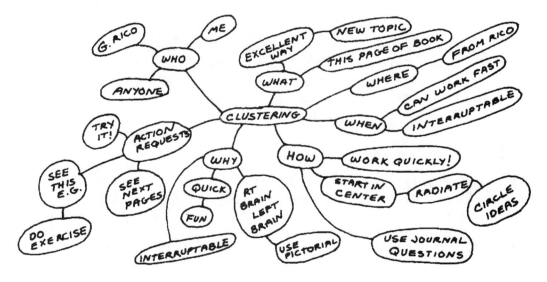

Clustering example

An exercise to help you practice cluster brainstorming is available for you to download from the Axzo Press Web site.

2. "Sticky-Note" Brainstorming

For a technique that can be useful for team brainstorming as well as individual brainstorming, try using sticky notes. First, individual brainstorming:

How to Use Sticky Notes for Individual Brainstorming

1. Get a pad of sticky notes, a pen, and one or two sheets of blank paper.

2. Write the topic of your brainstorming on the top of one of the sheets.

3. Start brainstorming by writing your first idea on a sticky note.

4. Put the sticky note anywhere on the paper that has the topic name.

5. Write more ideas down, one per sticky note, and put them on the paper. Use the brainstorming attitude: work fast, keep going, and don't organize or edit.

6. After a few minutes, stop and rest.

7. Make categories out of the brainstormed ideas by moving the sticky notes into columns of ideas that seem to belong together. Use the second paper, if you need more columns.

8. Label each column with a name that summarizes its content. If a name doesn't fit right away, that's OK; you might have too many ideas in some of your columns. Split the column into two or three new columns, and try labeling them again.

Your brainstorming might end up looking something like the example on the next page, especially if you organize with the brainstorming form available for download on the Axzo Press Web site. The columns of raw brainstorming ideas are lined up vertically, ready to be placed in a final order to serve as an outline for "Aerobic Writing" (see Tip 19).

Sticky-Note Brainstorming in Teams

Sticky-note brainstorming works well for teams, too. For teams, use flipcharts instead of sheets of paper. Everyone gets a pad of sticky notes and writes their ideas as fast as they can—one idea per note—and puts them anywhere on the flipchart.

Have everyone say their ideas out loud while they brainstorm. This tends to stimulate new ideas and makes the whole activity noisy and lively.

After a few minutes of brainstorming, have everyone just walk up to the flipchart and start putting the sticky notes into categories. Amazingly, this process can work well with several people working at once on the same chart—as long as they keep talking and negotiating while they organize and create category names.

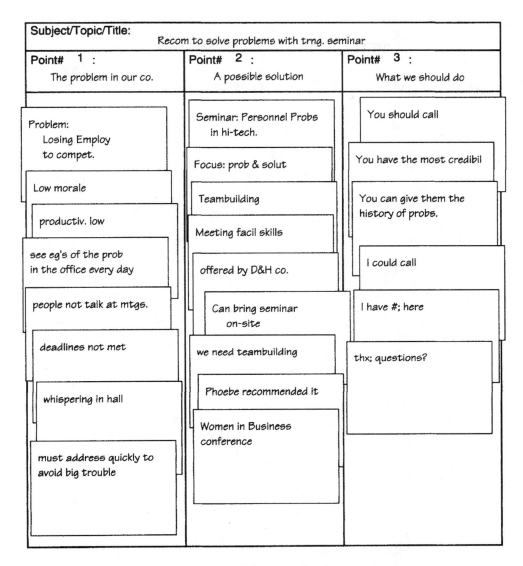

An example of sticky-note brainstorming

Electronic Sticky Notes

You can use a hard copy of the brainstorming form to place your sticky-notes ideas. Or if you prefer, you can type right into the on-screen form and use Cut and Paste to organize your ideas.

As an alternative method, some writers I know use Excel to brainstorm right into the cells of a spreadsheet, and then move ideas around to organize them.

Also, the program MindManager Pro simulates a combination of cluster and sticky-note brainstorming, and lets you link directly to Microsoft Word to finish your document.

3. Section Brainstorming for Long Documents

To get started writing long documents, break the task into manageable chunks by using section brainstorming. (FYI, I wrote this book by using this method.)

How to Use Section Brainstorming

1. Brainstorm a list of the names of sections (or paragraphs or chapters) the report will contain. Use previous reports as models if you wish. (Having sections labeled "Summary" and "Action Requests" is usually a good idea.)

2. Use one page of paper for each section named on your brainstormed list.

3. Pick up any of the section pages and start brainstorming ideas that will appear in that section. Use a brainstorming attitude (see Tip 17). Use clustering, keyword listing (as in the example below), or any other type of brainstorming you want. Skip around among section pages as ideas occur.

Here's an example of section brainstorming for a memo that will be entitled "Recommendation to implement the A-POWR writing process." Notice that the sections are in no particular order—we're just brainstorming, not organizing yet.

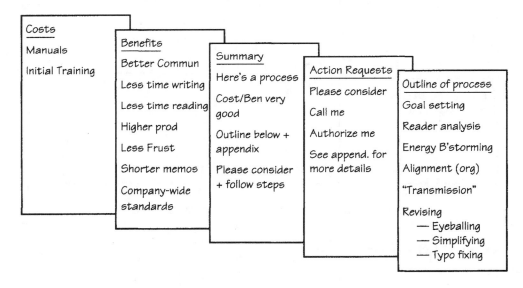

For Team Authorship, Use Flipcharts

To adapt section brainstorming to team-authorship projects, use blank flipchart pages instead of sheets of paper for report sections. Place the pages around the room and let team members wander about and add brainstorming ideas as they wish.

Tip 18: Put First Things First—And Last

Businesspeople don't always read every word of every e-mail message or document they get. Surprised? Probably not.

Like most professionals, you're probably swamped with information; you probably scan incoming documents to see if they're relevant enough to read fully. So how would you scan the sample hard-copy memo below?

A typical sequence would be to start with section A, and move to B, and then E. Then, based on what you find, you might go to sections C and D. If you don't read the rest of the memo, you're not lazy; you're just busy, and you're prioritizing on the fly.

INTEROFFICE MEMO

To: DeWitt Myway, Supervisor
From: Juan N. Olivus
Date: 2-7-2011   **A**
Subject: Recommendation to implement the
          GREATR writing process

Lorem ipsum dolor sit amet, consectetur adipiscing elit. Praesent
urna est, consequat ut mattis quis, consequat eu erat. Mauris ac   **B**
tortor consectetur libero tempus rhoncus in vitae lectus.

Maecenas lobortis elit vitae arcu malesuada condimentum. Lorem
ipsum dolor sit amet, consectetur adipiscing elit. Nunc fermentum
dui ac velit bibendum rutrum. Cras blandit facilisis leo ut hendrerit.
Vestibulum in felis felis. Mauris pharetra faucibus elit sit amet   **C**
sagittis. Pellentesque sit amet lacus mi, a lobortis neque. Nunc
luctus semper massa non ullamcorper.

Aliquam congue pharetra auctor. Pellentesque in felis id lacus
suscipit porta quis ut metus. Maecenas quis vestibulum nulla.
Donec sed quam sapien. Nullam nec erat nibh. Pellentesque ornare
rhoncus nisl non dictum. Praesent fringilla diam sed mi sagittis id
laoreet urna mattis. Mauris vitae augue non lacus volutpat   **D**
vestibulum eget pellentesque nibh. Morbi aliquam, velit vel
consequat dictum, eros nulla elementum orci, vel tempus lacus
ligula sit amet diam. Donec venenatis tristique vehicula.

Nulla euismod dui sed nunc tristique ullamcorper non vitae erat:
          — Vestibulum vel mauris felis
          — Non aliquet diam
          — Nullam congue   **E**
          — Nisi at mattis gravida

For Hard Copy, First and Last Are Critical...

Busy readers tend to notice the beginnings and ends of printed documents. So adapt to this; don't assume that what you write will be read in its entirety or in the order it appears in on the page. Instead, place must-see information at these strategic first and last locations on the page, and place details in the middle paragraphs.

...but in E-mail, Put Everything Important First

Treat e-mail messages differently from documents that will be read in hard copy. Most e-mail messages are visible on the screen in segments roughly equal to half a printed page. So write the two most important parts of your message—the summary and the action requests—on the first half-page. To be sure both parts are seen in the first view, put them in 1-2 order at the top of the message, and then put all the details underneath. Also:

▶ Use full, informative subject lines to grab the reader's interest.

▶ Put an executive summary, written in layman's terms, at position A.

▶ Put action requests—what you want the reader to do—at position B.

▶ To facilitate scanning, use headings to label each section of the document.

Use predictable formats for your e-mail messages and documents. Predictability will not only make your writing easier, but will give your regular readers easy-to-scan text.

A Collection of E-mail Templates

Consider using the formats below as templates for organizing your business e-mail messages. (These formats and several others are available on the Axzo Press Web site.) Notice how the formats provide summaries and action items in locations the readers are most likely to see.

Purpose: To recommend solutions to a problem	Purpose: To recommend a strategy to reach a goal	Purpose: To motivate to action
To From Date Subject	To From Date Subject	To From Date Subject
Summary	Summary	Summary
Action requests	Action requests	Action requests
(Optional) Summary of the problem and recommended solution(s)	The goal: a. Specific description of goal b. Benefits of goal	Consequences of inaction
The problem in detail: a. Negative effects b. Causes	Obstacles to goal	Comparison of possible actions
Comparison of possible solutions	Comparison of possible strategies to overcome obstacles	Recommended action: a. Specific benefits b. Specific features
Recommended solution(s)	Recommended strategy	Recommended first steps

Remember that to ensure easy scanning or reading, provide headings above each section of the e-mail message.

Experiment freely with these formats, and when you discover ones that work well—ones that make writing and reading easy—save them and use them.

A Template to Brainstorm E-mail Messages

You can brainstorm your own easy-to-read e-mail messages by making a full-size version of this simple template.

Type or handwrite the template on 8.5"×11" paper and make several copies.

To brainstorm an e-mail message, just scribble some bullet points (or place sticky-note ideas) right on a printout of the template. Then quickly sequence the ideas, type them up on screen, remember to include informative headings, and you're writing— quickly and well.

To:
From:
Date:
Subject:

Summary:

Action Requests:

Details:

Tip 19: Practice "Aerobic Writing"

If you exercise to stay physically fit, you know that continuity is important. It's the same with "aerobic writing." Just as you wouldn't stop in mid-workout to take a shower and then resume working out, you shouldn't stop aerobic writing to tidy up your language. Instead, trust yourself. You can do the good grooming later, after the real workout.

If you stop to edit too soon, you'll interrupt yourself—your creative mind will defer to your editorial mind—and you may not get your creative flow back.

Some Aerobic Writing Techniques

▶ Use your brainstormed outline as a guide.

▶ Make a conscious effort to keep going and avoid editing.

▶ If you know you've made a grammatical mistake, misspelled a word, or written an awkward phrase, just mark it with a short line of X's. Then forget it and keep going. You'll easily find it and fix it later.

▶ If you're a good typist, consider "invisible writing"—typing with your screen either turned off or blocked by a sheet of paper—so you won't be tempted to look at and edit your writing too soon.

▶ If you have writer's block, try clustering your ideas. Or pretend you're talking to a buddy, saying, "The idea is simple—what I mean is…" and talking the idea out. Then write down what you said.

The most important principle is keep going and don't worry. Give yourself a productive writing workout now; clean it up later.

Suggestions for Reducing Writing Distractions

Writing business documents, like any high-concentration activity, is much easier if you can work uninterrupted. A one-minute interruption from a writing task might require as much as 20 minutes of recovery time before you can resume the flow. Try some of these ideas to reduce the distractions to your aerobic writing:

1. **Come in early or stay late.**
   Or go to lunch a half-hour later. Use the relatively quiet time just after noon.

2. **Schedule writing appointments with yourself.**
   If someone asks to see you during your scheduled time, say "Sorry, I have an appointment. What other time would be good for you?"

3. **Hang a "Do Not Disturb Until…" or "In Conference Until…" sign on your door.**

4. **Turn your writing space away from the entrance to your workspace.**

   Especially if you have no office door, turning away from the entrance to your office space will reduce your interruptions.

5. **Use white noise.**

   In noisy and open offices, play a radio softly or run a small fan to minimize distracting conversations floating over your partition.

6. **Make your office temporarily less inviting to visitors.**

   Sit in front of a bright window, put books on visitors' chairs, or remove visitors' chairs altogether.

7. **Ignore the phone if you can.**

   Turn off your cell phone or set it to vibrate. Or forward your calls or ask someone to screen them. Take your desk phone off the hook to signal that you're busy—which you are.

8. **Promise callbacks.**

   If you're writing and someone calls or pops in, quickly say, "Can I get back to you in about 15 minutes?" Then immediately get back to writing.

9. **Find a "writing-hiding" place.**

   Try an empty office, an unoccupied conference room, a storeroom, or even a stall in the lavatory or your car in the parking lot. I know professionals who claim success with each of these writing-hiding places!

10. **Have an office "quiet time."**

    If possible, try to institute an office "quiet time"; that is, a time when internal phone calls, meetings, and visits are curtailed, except for emergencies. The quiet time doesn't have to be very long—perhaps 9:30 to 10:00 on Tuesdays and Thursdays.

However you do it, minimize your writing distractions. Especially if you're using aerobic writing, an uninterrupted half hour can be very productive.

Tip 20: Use "Big-Middle-Little" Revising

Revising is challenging because writing is challenging. Written language involves issues of word choice, tone, punctuation, spelling, organization, connectivity, formality, ambiguity, visual formatting, sequence of tenses, pronoun agreement, conciseness, and adaptation to audience—to name just a few. All of these factors are complex systems of constantly evolving linguistic conventions.

Wait, are we supposed to remember all that at once as we revise our writing? No way. That's why we should break up revising into three manageable chunks.

To Simplify the Task: Big-Middle-Little Revising

A good way to revise is do it more than once, looking only for certain factors each time. I recommend using the "big-middle-little" approach:

1. **Big revising** — Skim through your document, looking for the big picture—the overall content and organization of your work. Eyeball the text from a distance: Does it look easy to read (with lots of white space, clearly marked sections, and so on), or does it look like a brick wall of unbroken words? If a memo looks hard to read, it is hard to read, and it may not be read at all.

2. **Middle revising** — Next, quickly read for simplicity, clarity, and conciseness. Do your readers absolutely need to know everything you've written? Can you leave phrases, paragraphs, or even whole sections out? Can you simplify the language in what's left? Are your ideas clear and to the point?

3. **Little revising** — Next, look for the details: the grammar, spelling, and punctuation. Leave these small but very important details for last. Why correct the spelling of a word you might end up eliminating?

This Book's Emphasis: Big Revising

The "middle" and "little" levels are where you're likely to get the most help from spelling checkers, traditional style guides, or eagle-eyed colleagues, so the next few pages will focus mostly on the often-neglected aspects of "big" revising.

But don't neglect any levels of revising—remember that when you write, your credibility is on the line. Try big-middle-little revising. It's much more effective than trying to see everything at once.

Tip 21: Add "Breathing Space" for Reader Friendliness

When you first revise your writing, starting with "big" revising, consider adding "breathing space." Spread out your written information so that it looks easy to read and so your reader can find your main ideas quickly.

Breathing Space in Writing: A True Story

A few years ago an old friend decided to start a new life. He just picked up and moved from Chicago to Phoenix. He arrived, wrote up a résumé—a one-pager, crammed edge-to-edge with everything he'd ever done—and started looking for work. Months went by—no job. Puzzled and worried, he revamped his résumé, spreading out the same information over two pages, making the pages more open and easy to read.

The next week he found work. What happened? Somebody finally read his résumé.

The Bottom Line: Revise for Reader Friendliness

The moral of this story applies to all business writing: Revise your documents to look reader friendly and pleasing to the eye. Make your key information easy to find. Add breathing space with:

▶ **Frequent paragraph breaks** — You can even use occasional one- or two-line paragraphs for important thoughts.

▶ **Lists** — Readers find listed information easier to organize, so they look at lists almost immediately. Lists can also condense documents by allowing the use of phrases instead of sentences.

▶ **Wide margins** — Readers find shorter text lines easier to read than long, edge-to-edge text lines, and wide margins give readers more room for writing notes.

▶ **Section headings** — Headings allow readers to scan for main ideas, read selectively or in any order they wish, and easily review the document at a later time. Bonus: Headings help the document appeal to readers with different interests. Technical people can go right to the section marked "Technical Data," while others may skip to "Cost/Benefit Analysis."

Every business document you write competes for your reader's precious time. Busy readers may not even look at documents that look difficult. So when you revise your work, make sure to add enough breathing space to make it reader friendly.

WHICH WOULD YOU RATHER READ?

Read the document below.

> *To: DeWitt Myway, Supervisor*
> *From: Juan N. Olivus*
> *Date: 2 February 2011*
> *Subject: Writing*
>
> *The A-POWR writing process consists of five easy steps: analyzing goals and readers; producing ideas through brainstorming; organizing ideas; writing the draft; and then revising for organization, clarity, and accuracy. The benefits we would gain are many and the total cost of the program compared to what we would gain is minimal. Our company would enjoy total savings of between $1500 and $10,000 per year per employee. We would spend about 30%–50% less time writing and about 25% less time reading. We would definitely have better communication and therefore fewer misunderstandings and in addition we would have higher levels of trust among employees. Higher productivity would result because we would all be able to complete more projects in less time. We would also have company-wide standards by which to create and judge future documents. I recommend we implement this process in our office as soon as possible. Please consider this recommendation, call me if you have any questions or need more information, and authorize me to implement the process in our office. If you concur with my recommendation, please consider these action requests. The process itself has five relatively easy steps, which I've outlined in this memo. The benefits we would accrue from this program are many. The cost of the program involves only manuals and initial training. So the total investment we would have to make in the program per employee would be only about $200.*

Did you actually read through the whole document? Probably not—few people ever do.

Notice the difference between this document and the second version of it. The second version uses the "breathing space" techniques of paragraph breaks, lists, widened margins, headings, and a simpler font. It also uses a fuller, more complete subject line.

Oddly enough, the second version takes more space on the page—in a way, you could say it's "longer"—but really, which one is easier to read? If you prefer the second version, perhaps you agree that a document's length is not as important to readers as its breathing space.

CONTINUED

To: DeWitt Myway, Supervisor
From: Juan N. Olivus
Date: 2 Feb 2011
Subject: Recommendation that we train our staff in the
A-POWR Writing Process

Summary

I recommend that you let me bring our staff a training program in the A-POWR Writing Process. The benefits we would gain are many and the total cost of the program is minimal. The writing process itself has five relatively easy steps, which I've outlined below.

The Benefits of the A-POWR Writing Process

The benefits we would enjoy from the training are:

--Less time writing. The process saves 30–50% of writing time.
--Less time reading. Estimated savings: 25%,
--Total time savings equivalent to between $1500 and $10,000 per employee per year.
--Better communication and fewer misunderstandings among employees, resulting in higher levels of trust and better morale.
--Higher productivity. More projects can be completed in less time.
--Company-wide standards by which to create and judge future documents.

Program Costs: $200 Per Employee

Program costs involve only manuals and initial training. Our total investment would be about $200 per employee.

Outline of the A-POWR Writing Process

The process itself consists of five easy steps:
1. Analyze your goals and readers.
2. Produce ideas through brainstorming.
3. Organize the ideas.
4. Write a draft of the document.
5. Revise for organization, clarity, and accuracy.

Action Requests

Please consider this recommendation, call me if you have any questions or need more information, and authorize me to implement the process in our office.

Tip 22: Make Subject Lines and Headings Longer, Not Shorter

What? Longer? Isn't conciseness the great Gold Standard of business writing? No, not always. Not when it comes to subject lines and headings.

If today's front-page headline read "Supreme Court," you'd say "Why do I have to read the article to get the main point?" The same goes for subject lines of e-mail messages and documents. For example: "Board Meeting." What is this message's point? Is it an invitation? An agenda? You can't tell; you'd have to keep reading. This vague subject line wastes your time; because it's so short, it's almost useless.

Informative Subject Lines: Purpose Plus Topic

To make your subject lines more clear, think: Subject line = Purpose + Topic. For example: "Request to cancel next management meeting." This "headline" is instantly clear because it states the memo's purpose ("Request to cancel") and then the topic ("next management meeting"). Another clear one: "Summary of revisions to design of XYZ." Purpose: To summarize revisions. Topic: Design of XYZ.

The "purpose" component of a good subject line can appear in several forms: "Update on," "Recommendation to," "Outline of," "Schedule for," "Proposal to," and so on. The "topic" component can refer to anything under the sun.

Another way to make subject lines more complete is to write them as full sentences ("Please cancel the management meeting") or as titles ("How We Revised the XYZ Design"). These are unusual subject lines, but they are effective. They communicate a whole idea, like a good newspaper headline.

As one of the steps in big revising, try improving your subject lines. Doing so will make your memos more focused, more readable—and instantly clear.

Incomplete Subject Line	**Complete Subject Lines**
To: DeWitt Myway From: Juan N. Olivus Date: 2 Feb 2011 Subject: Writing	To: DeWitt Myway From: Juan N. Olivus Date: 2 Feb 2011 Subject: Recommendation that we get training in A-POWR Writing (or) Subject: We should all be trained in A-POWR Writing

If It's All in the Subject Line, use "EOM"

"EOM" (or "eom" or "<eom>" or "[eom]") means "end of message." If you can write the whole message in the subject line, "EOM" tells the reader "That's it; no need to open the e-mail message." Use the EOM technique whenever you can.

Use Expanded, Informative Headings

Using headings is one of the smartest things a business writer can do. Here's why:

Headings Help Writers Stay Organized

Headings almost force writers to be well organized. When a memo has headings, topics don't wander because everything has to be put into clearly labeled sections. Also, as we discussed in Tip 21, headings allow writers to address different types of readers in the same document. Headings also help a writer to check whether the major sections of her work are in the right order.

Even Basic Headings Help Readers Read Selectively

Readers like headings because they can find important ideas like "Summary," "Financial Implications," or "Action Items" right away; they can read document sections in whatever order they want, just like they read a newspaper; and they won't waste time reading 80% of a document to find the 20% that interests them.

Expanded Headings Can Summarize Whole Messages

Look at the examples below. The basic headings on the left are OK—much better than no headings at all. But look at the ones on the right; they tell whole stories. They let busy readers skim and scan and still get the idea. But they don't prevent readers who want details from reading them.

Basic Headings	More Informative Headings
Introduction	Introduction: The Problem of Airflow Management
Background	Background: Present System Al Mostly Obsolete
Upgrade Costs	Cost of Upgrade Prohibitive at $250K
Recommendation	Recommendation: New System Will Save Long-Term $$

Incidentally, did you notice the headings on this page? If you read just these headings, without the paragraphs they accompany, you still get the message, right?

When you write and revise, aim for conciseness almost everywhere—except in your headings and subject lines.

Try the exercise called "Effective Subject Lines," available for download from the Axzo Press Web site.

Tip 23: Simplify and Clarify Your Document

"Middle"-level revising means improving the conciseness and clarity of your writing. To do middle revising well, develop the attitude that the right words are the simplest words that work. Here are a couple other attitudes or ways of thinking that will help you revise:

▶ Write to express, not impress. The purpose of business writing should be not to show off, but to inform. Pompous writing alienates busy readers.

▶ Write as if your readers were 12 years old. If this sounds like stupid advice, consider this quote from Albert Einstein: "Everything should be made as simple as possible, but not simpler."

Some Techniques That Will Help You Revise

▶ **Reduce or eliminate big words.** Beware of three-, four-, and five syllable words. Change "Our contemporary organizational structure possesses the prerequisite autonomous functioning capability" to "Today we have the strength we need to stand alone." Some technical words may be necessary, but always try to use the simplest words that work.

▶ **Use personal pronouns.** Instead of, "It is recommended that this procedure be implemented," write, "We recommend that you implement this procedure." Personal pronouns can help make sentences simpler, less abstract, and more personal. They also clarify the important issue of who does what.

▶ **Ask the "Big Question."** If your writing is too complex or wordy, read it over and ask the "big question," which is "What does that mean?" That is, think about the basic meaning of what you have just read—not the individual words or grammatical structures—and then just restate that meaning as a clear, concise, simply worded idea.

In using the "Ask the 'Big Question'" technique, you revise by speaking aloud, not by editing on the page. For example, imagine that you have just explained an idea to someone, but he says he didn't quite follow it. What would you do? You wouldn't recompose the idea with a pencil in hand; you would probably just describe the idea again, in simpler language. That's how you use the "big question" technique. Read the wordy passage and ask yourself "What does that mean?" Then restate it in simpler terms.

For practice with this technique, try the exercise on the next page.

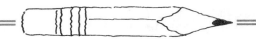

ASKING THE "BIG QUESTION"

Use the big-question technique to reduce the wordy sentences below to the fewest, simplest words possible. Read each sentence, look away from the page, ask, "What does that mean?" and say the revision. Then write it down. Count the words in your revision to see how well you did.

You can download copies of this exercise from the Axzo Press Web site.

1. "We are in the process of formulating an attempt to articulate a policy that will be characterized by a complete and comprehensive inclusiveness of all parties." (26 words)

_____

_____

_____

2. "Should you have the occasion to know or make the acquaintance of any person whose professional background configuration approximates the position description, we would welcome receiving a notification from you or directly from the individual who is exploring the position opportunity." (41 words)

_____

_____

_____

3. "As soon as you're able to lay your hands on the information on the project, the latest stuff you have, do you think you can send it over to me in the earliest possible time frame? I really have a desire to go through it with a fine-tooth comb and see what there is to see. After I'm done reading it, perhaps you and I could talk or e-mail or meet and ask and answer any questions either of us have. Is that OK with you?" (87 words)

_____

_____

_____

Compare your answers with the author's suggested responses
in the Appendix.

Tip 24: After You Check Spelling, Proofread

The third level of revising, "little" revising, means ensuring that your document has good grammar, mechanics, and spelling. Some spelling-and-grammar checkers (like the one in Microsoft Word) are useful, and others are not as good (Microsoft PowerPoint's grammar checker isn't as robust).

Even good checkers will not catch some mistakes, like "manger" for "manager," "mane" for "name," or "clock" for "click," so try the proofreading techniques described here.

Before You Proofread

Run your software's spelling checker first. Let it find whatever it can.

Shift the format of the document. Change the font, the text color, the margins, the spacing—anything to change the document's appearance. Your brain will "wake up" to anything that looks new and different.

Print the document. You'll be amazed how much more attention you'll pay to it.

Take a break before revising. Wait for an hour, or a whole day if possible. Let your brain do something else, and then you can come back fresh.

When You Proofread

Choose an "awake" time in your day. For many people, the best time is late morning. But people are different. When are you most alert? That's when to revise.

Consider reading the document out loud. This may slow you down enough to notice things you'd miss otherwise.

Consider "progressive revelation." Over your printed document, slowly pull down a blank sheet, revealing one line at a time. This is an old proofreading trick.

Consider "reverse reading." This is "progressive revelation" in reverse. Reading backwards, your mind can't read thoughts; it sees only words and letters. This technique works beautifully for detecting spelling errors and typos.

For critical documents, consider "focused proofreading." This means reading through the document several times: once just for spelling and typos, once just for grammar, and once just for punctuation.

After You Proofread

Ask someone else to proofread your work (see Tip 25) if the document is critical.

Then look through your work one last time. Ask yourself honestly "Is this the best I can do?"

(For a good proofreading challenge, download the Proofreading Challenge exercise on the Axzo Press Web site.)

Tip 25: How to Comment on Each Other's Writing

Showing your work to another person, or reviewing somebody else's work, can be an uncomfortable experience. An honest critique can be difficult to give or receive, especially since "critique" sounds like "criticism," a word that connotes negative feedback. A better word for a review process is "commentary," and following a few guidelines can make the process more smooth and productive.

Commentary Guidelines

Choose peer reviewers. Choose reviewers who are on your level in the organization. If you ask supervisors to review your work, you might think their comments are orders, not suggestions. If you ask subordinates, they might not speak freely enough.

Tell reviewers what to look for. Ask commentators to be especially aware of your document's accuracy, or organization, or visual appeal, or conciseness, or grammar—whatever factors you think might need the most work. Being specific is much better than just asking them to "look this over."

Be helpful. When commenting on others' work, remember that your goal is to help colleagues, not just find their mistakes. Have a good heart about your task.

Speak concisely. Make your comments concise. Don't justify every comment unless the writer asks for your reasons. When you are receiving commentary, don't get defensive. Simply listen, without trying to justify what you wrote. Then decide later which review comments are valid.

Speak in compliments and suggestions. When commenting, say what you liked about the document, and then make suggestions for improvements. Don't confuse suggestions with complaints. Instead of saying, "I can't figure out what you mean here" or "This page is too hard to read," say, "I suggest simplifying the language here" and "You might make the margins wider and put in a heading between paragraphs 2 and 3."

Tip 26: E-mail Time Savers and Etiquette Points

Writing and Sending E-mail Messages

▶ **Choose your recipients with care.** Plan to send copies to only those people who absolutely, positively need the message.

▶ **Know how to brainstorm.** Many good writers brainstorm on paper first, perhaps even using a form like the one at the end of Tip 18. Then they type the e-mail message. What works best for you?

▶ **Be careful about using "stationery" letterhead or pages with backgrounds.** They use a lot of memory and they might not even show up well.

▶ **Use large, easy-to-read fonts.**

▶ **Avoid typing in all capitals—or all lowercase.** ALL CAPS SURE LOOKS LIKE SHOUTING, DOESN'T IT? Also, writing without standard capitalization inhibits the recognition of acronyms, proper names, and sentence beginnings, all of which depend on upper- and lowercase contrasts.

▶ **If you can't keep it short, forecast its structure.** On your readers' first screen, summarize your message and forecast its structure by listing your section headings. This helps readers scroll to sections that interest them.

▶ **Use formatting devices and highlighting.** Headings, white space, lists, boldface, and underlining help readers find ideas fast.

▶ **Use colors to highlight, but be careful about reds and greens.** Red/green color blindness is common, affecting about 9% of all males.

▶ **Be conservative with "text-y" acronyms and "emoticons."** Only some people like seeing "LOL" and ☺. When in doubt, don't use them.

▶ **Send e-mail messages right the first time.** Ever forget to send the attachment? Me, too. Try this: Put the attachment in first, then write the text, and then select recipients. Doing this seems backwards, but it works.

Reading and Responding to E-mail

▶ **Scan the subject lines of all your messages before you open any.** This helps you to prioritize and to detect any "ignore my last e-mail" messages.

▶ **If you receive a message by mistake, notify the sender right away.**

▶ **Print long messages to increase your skim/scan reading options.** Scanning hard copy for sections is easier than scrolling on a screen.

▶ **Reply quickly.** More and more people expect replies sooner and sooner. Reply in 24 hours or less.

▶ **Be careful not to overuse high-priority sending features, like "!" in Outlook.** If everything is critical, nothing is critical. Some good writers recommend never using the "!"; they recommend using informative subject lines instead.

▶ **When replying, change the end of the subject line to reflect the new message.** Reply to "Project X Update" with "Re: Project X Update: 3 questions." Preserving the front of the subject line will make archiving the e-mail easier.

▶ **To avoid huge volumes of e-mail, be careful about using "Reply to All."**

Be "E-mail Smart"

▶ **Be careful with confidential subjects.** Who knows where your messages will be forwarded?

▶ **Assume readers you don't know have high standards.** Many readers are put off by careless writing in any form. Write right!

▶ **Be aware of what your readers think of receipt notification and blind copies.** These can be useful features, but some readers may find them overbearing, sneaky, or both.

▶ **Consider listing multiple recipients alphabetically.** Names are easier to find on alphabetized lists. Also, sometimes people wonder why they're last on unalphabetized lists—or why they're not first. The alphabetizing minimizes the politics of rank.

▶ **Consider the cost/benefit of cuteness.** Some people really like getting motivational stories, precious pictures, and extra "Thank you/You're welcome" messages. But some people don't like them at all. If you're unsure, don't send the cuteness.

Tip 27: Format Points for Technical Reports

▶ When writing technical documents, use large margins, especially if your work might be e-mailed and opened in different formats (PDF, HTML, and so on).

▶ In paragraphs, put your main points first whenever possible.

▶ If possible, break long procedures into several tasks with no more than nine steps per task.

▶ To make for easier searching through a long hard-copy document, put page numbers in the lower outside corners of pages.

▶ Use continuous page numbers throughout a multi-chapter document. Do not use the "chapter-page" numbering format (e.g., 2-7, 2-8, 2-9, and so on).

▶ Don't hard-code (type by hand) your document's table of contents, caption numbers, and cross-references. Rather, let your desktop publishing software create them so they will be easier to update.

▶ Note that several popular technical writing templates use the Arial font for headers, footers, and headings, but Times New Roman for everything else, as shown in the following example.

PROCEDURES FOR QUALIFIED PARTICIPANTS

If you qualify for the study, we will guide you through several procedures. If you agree to participate, you will be asked to sign a consent form. We will answer any questions you have about the form before you sign it. During a screening visit, we will record your general medical history. Also, we will check your vision and tear function, and examine the front of your eyes with a microscope.

▶ If possible, write short paragraphs and use subheadings, as shown in the following example.

PROCEDURES FOR QUALIFIED PARTICIPANTS

If you qualify for the study, we will guide you through several procedures:

<u>Giving your consent.</u> If you agree to participate, you will be asked to sign a consent form. We will answer any questions you have about the form before you sign it.

<u>Medical screening.</u> During a screening visit, we will record your general medical history. Also, we will check your vision and tear function, and examine the front of your eyes with a microscope.

▶ Add indented and bold section summaries below the headings of long sections, as shown in the following example.

PROCEDURES FOR QUALIFIED PARTICIPANTS

> **Summary. After you sign a consent form, we will screen your medical history. If you are female, we will give you a pregnancy test. Then we will put drops in your eyes, ask you to watch TV in a special chamber, and run several tests on your eyes.**

If you qualify for the study, we will guide you through several procedures:

<u>Giving your consent.</u> If you agree to participate, you will be asked to sign a consent form. We will answer any questions you have about the form before you sign it.

<u>Medical screening.</u> During a screening visit, we will record your general medical history. Also, we will check your vision and tear function, and examine the front of your eyes with a microscope.

▶ Check for consistency in your document's:

1. Page layouts. Ensure that:

    — All page headers and footers are accurate and correctly positioned

    — Headings are consistent in capitalization, typeface, and highlighting

    — Chapter openings are always on the right-side page

2. Formatting of tables, screen shots, and other visuals. Review their:

    — Alignments within the text

    — Relation to page breaks

3. Vertical alignments, including:

    — Margins

    — Paragraph justifications

    — Lists and bullet points

    — Procedure-step decimal points

4. Format numbers, including:

    — Overall pagination

    — Tables of contents

    — Indexes

5. Typefaces. Ensure the consistency of:

    — Fonts

    — Size

    — Spaces between words

Tip 28: Write Clear Action Steps in Procedures

Do not bunch actions within one step. Give each action its own step:

Ineffective	Effective
1. Level the device against the wall. Make sure the wires will feed through the opening. Mark the mounting hole locations.	1. Level the device against the wall. 2. Make sure the wires will feed through the opening. 3. Mark the mounting hole locations.

Do not use ambiguous passive-voice sentences. Either use the word "you" or use imperative (also called "you-understood" or "you-active") sentences:

Ineffective	Effective
If two-transformer wiring is used in the device, it should be in phase.	If you use two-transformer wiring in the device, make sure it is in phase. (or) 1. Select two-transformer wiring for the device. 2. Before you install the wiring, make sure it is in phase.

Be aware of action sequences. Describe activities in the order the user will experience them in:

Ineffective	Effective
1. Select YES from the VOICE INSTRUCTION menu. Set the time and temperature by following the voice instructions.	1. From the VOICE INSTRUCTION menu, select YES. 2. Following the voice instructions, set the time and temperature.

In warning messages, place the warning before the step; then name the risk.
Be especially careful to follow user sequences:

Ineffective	Effective
Danger! Switch on the unit after ensuring it is grounded.	Danger! Risk of electrocution. Ensure that the unit is grounded before you switch it on.

Use consistent terms:

Ineffective	Effective
1. Click on CHANGE PROGRAM. 2. Select YES. 3. Click on WEEKDAY. 4. Choose YES.	1. Select CHANGE PROGRAM. 2. Select YES. 3. Select WEEKDAY. 4. Select YES.

Use the "step-action" format to distinguish user actions from system reactions.
When describing system reactions, prefer the present tense to the future tense:

Ineffective	Effective
1. When you press the RUN button, the system will display COMPLETE.	1. Press the RUN button. The system displays COMPLETE.

The A-POWR Writing Process

1. Analyze your goals and readers. To avoid the Specialist's Fallacy (Tip 29), use a Document Planner Page (Tip 16) to adapt to:

    a. Your readers' level of knowledge;

    b. Their needs and attitudes;

    c. What you want them to know and feel;

    d. What actions you want from them;

    e. Their communication styles;

    f. How and how much they will read.

2. Produce your ideas with brainstorming (Tip 17).

    a. Write fast! Include all ideas! Don't edit!

    b. Use one or more brainstorm techniques: clustering, sticky notes, or section frames.

3. Organize your ideas (Tip 18).

    a. Position important ideas:

        i. First in e-mail messages;

        ii. First and last in documents.

    b. Make use of ready-made templates (Tip 18).

4. Write your draft.

    a. Use Aerobic Writing (Tip 19).

        i. Write quickly!

        ii. Write without editing; keep going!

        iii. Manage writer's block.

    b. With e-mail, use time savers and etiquette points (Tip 26).

5. Revise systematically (Tip 20).

    a. First, organization and format:

        i. Ensure a reader-friendly format (Tip 21).

        ii. Write informative subject lines and expanded headings (Tip 22).

    b. Second, clarity and conciseness (Tip 23):

        i. Omit wordiness and redundancy.

        ii. Ask the Big Question: "What does that mean?"

    c. Third, mechanical accuracy (Tip 24):

        i. Run spelling and grammar checkers.

        ii. Proofread for:

            ▷ Confusing words, hard spellings, and typos;

            ▷ Grammar—fragments, run-ons, references, parallelism;

            ▷ Punctuation—commas, apostrophes, and so on.

    d. Follow guidelines for giving and receiving feedback on writing (Tip 25).

Fourteen Tips to Improve Your Presentations

Fourteen Tips to Improve Your Presentations

To find out how good your presentations are, ask your colleagues to observe a presentation you give and fill out the "How Do You Present?" form, available for downloading from the Axzo Press Web site. You'll find out how you're doing in terms of organization, question answering, delivery skills, and visual aids. Then you can refer to the appropriate Tips in this book.

Organization

Tips 29–33 show you how to analyze audiences, earn an audience's attention in an introduction, use stories and "Fast Facts" to keep their attention, use the B.E.S.T. recipe to organize points, and leave listeners feeling involved and enthusiastic after you conclude.

Techniques for brainstorming the content of presentations, as well as written documents, constitute Tip 17.

Answering Questions

Tip 34 gives you strategies for answering questions in general, and suggests the Q-BEST-Q recipe when you need to give longer, more complex answers.

Delivery Skills

You will improve your gestures by trying the techniques in Tip 35. Tip 36 will help you improve your "voice music" by strengthening your projection, reducing the use of non-words like "um" and "uh," and liberating the "notes" of your voice. Tip 37 will help you master the important skill of making eye contact with your listeners.

Special Presentations

Tips 38–40 give you suggestions on how to do three kinds of special presentations: impromptu presentations, one-on-one sales presentations to VIPs, and team presentations.

Presenting Challenges

Tips 41 and 42 help you face two of the common challenges of presenting: recovering from mistakes and managing nervousness.

On the Axzo Press Web site is a special Bonus Tip, "How to Prepare a Presentation," which summarizes the process for creating the verbal part of business presentations.

Visual aids for business presentations are discussed in this book's next section, "Eight Tips for Using PowerPoint."

If you would like more information on presentation skills, see the Axzo Press book *Effective Presentations,* by Steve Mandel.

Tip 29: Plan to Speak to Listeners on Their Terms

Suppose you're an area manager for a wireless communications company. One day your five-year-old niece asks you, "Aunt Kathleen, what do you do at work?" You say something like, "Well, Natalie, I talk to people all day long to help them make phones! Like this one!" Good answer. Now suppose your boss wants a report on what you and your area have been up to lately. Would you give the same answer? Of course not—you would radically adjust your message to your new listener.

To communicate well, you shouldn't speak (or write) the same way to everybody, even if you're describing the same thing. You need to adjust your messages to your listeners. Some professionals create presentations or documents that are hard to follow exactly because they don't make this adjustment. These professionals may be suffering from a common communication malady I call the "Specialist's Fallacy."

▶ **The Specialist's Fallacy: How presentations go wrong** — The Specialist's Fallacy is a mistaken assumption that your listeners are (or should be) just as familiar with your subject as you are. If you assume this, you may lose your audience by giving talks that are too long, too detailed, and full of technical jargon. You may even find yourself getting impatient with listeners who "should know this stuff by now." Presentations given this way are easy to misunderstand and even easier to disregard.

▶ **Where the Specialist's Fallacy originates** — The Specialist's Fallacy comes from mistaking familiarity with a subject for an intrinsic simplicity of the subject. ("If I understand it, everyone understands it.") Oddly, even though many of us are highly specialized professionals, we may not appreciate how much we have learned in our fields. We underestimate ourselves, assuming that what we know is common knowledge and that everyone will understand us if we just say what we know. We have forgotten what it was like to have a "beginner's mind." So we speak or write in our specialist's terms to audiences who are specialists, too, but in other areas. The result: They don't understand us.

▶ **The Solution: Plan to speak to listeners on their own terms** — To avoid the Specialist's Fallacy and plan your presentations for your listeners, use the Presentation Planning Form available from the Axzo Press Web site. Filling out this form (and adjusting accordingly) will help you create talks that overcome the Specialist's Fallacy, tailor your message to your listeners, and communicate clearly.

Tip 30: Use a Recipe to Begin with Confidence

After planning, use brainstorming to create and roughly organize your whole talk, just as if you were writing a document. (See Tip 17, plus "How to Prepare a Presentation," available from the Axzo Press Web site.) Then start on your presentation's introduction.

To make your introductions work well, even when you're nervous, follow a good "recipe," a talking sequence you trust. If you do, you might still feel a bit nervous, but you'll have the confidence of knowing you're saying the right things.

Here's a tried-and-true recipe for a business presentation's introduction.

1. **Say hello and say your name.** Greet the audience with a strong, clear voice. If anyone in the audience doesn't know who you are, say your name. (If someone has introduced you, you don't have to say your name again.)

2. **Name your topic.** Tell them right away what you'll be discussing. If you're using a visual with the title of your talk, gesture to it as you announce your topic. (Don't trust the technique of starting with a joke. Humor is tricky; you're safest if you get right down to business and name the topic.)

3. **Give your topic credentials.** Pretend you're answering the question "How are you qualified in this topic?" Don't detail your whole résumé—just say enough to show your credibility in this topic. Don't brag; just state your experience in two or three sentences. (If someone has introduced you and already explained your background, you can omit this part.)

4. **Emphasize the benefits the audience will gain by listening to you.** This is a sometimes neglected but crucial part of an effective business presentation. (See the "Why Should They Listen to You?" exercise on the Axzo Press Web site.)

5. **Forecast the structure of your talk.** Briefly outline the agenda points you will cover. Don't detail them yet; just list them. If you're using visuals, show the audience a visual agenda to accompany your words.

6. **Suggest question-and-answer rules.** Tell the audience when you'd like them to ask their questions—anytime, after sections, or after the entire talk.

7. **Start agenda item #1.** Simply say, "Now let's start with point 1," and you're in. Now you can start detailing the points of your talk.

On the Axzo Press Web site is an Introduction Recipe document you can use to create an effective introduction.

Tip 31: To Build Credibility, Use Personal Stories and "Fast Facts"

Using personal stories and relevant facts in your presentations can help you keep your audience engaged.

Personal Stories Make Presenters "Real People"

In his book *Leading Out Loud*, author Terry Pearce shows us that leaders who are effective tend to be perceived by their teams as "real." One of the ways leaders communicate this authenticity is to tell personal stories in their presentations.

But personal stories shouldn't be used haphazardly. The stories should be:

▶ **True** — Don't pass off fiction as reality. If listeners find out you lied about a story, they'll wonder what else you lied about.

▶ **Relevant to the subject** — "Stories about nothing" may have worked on the TV show *Seinfeld*, but they probably won't work in your presentations. Unless you're Jerry Seinfeld.

▶ **Conversational** — Tell personal stories in an informal way. Don't rehearse them too much; they come across better if you use an off-the-cuff style.

▶ **About you** — Stories about others might work OK, but not as well as stories that reveal something about you.

▶ **Vivid** — Include a few relevant sight-and-sound details so that listeners can imagine the scene you describe.

▶ **Concise** — Even though you include details, try to keep each story fairly short. Remember, the story probably isn't the point; it just supports the point.

USE VIVID DETAILS IN STORIES

Think of a presentation you give, a point you make in the presentation, and a personal story to support that point. Fill in the boxes below, listing vivid sight- and sound details that will make the story effective.

Presentation:	Specific point:

Personal story details:

"Fast Facts" Build Credibility in Real Life…

Remember, years ago, that schoolteacher of yours who wrote a few words of Latin and Greek on the board one day? You were impressed: "Wow, Miss Fufufnik knows Latin and Greek!" Or remember when you met that new golf partner, watched him hit a great tee shot on the first hole, and assumed he was an excellent golfer?

We make judgments like these because we tend to generalize from specific experiences. We tend to assume, rightly or wrongly, that behind any specific behavior is a general pattern of knowledge, skill, or similar behavior.

…and in Presentations

Something similar happens in presentations. If you give your audience specific names, facts, examples, statistics, stories, or analogies—especially lots of them in a rapid-fire sequence—the audience is likely to assume that for each specific, you could have said even more. "If that's the case," they think to themselves, "this presenter's evidence is overwhelming. His point must be valid."

Think "Many and Quick"

Listeners often respond this way to many specifics quickly stated. Another reason listeners respond positively is that they hear quick specifics as a wide sweep, an overview of the evidence. And providing a clear, concise, comprehensive overview is an impressive feat.

But listeners may eventually require more depth, so a good presentation strategy might be to give the quick specifics, and then go back and develop just a few of your specifics in detail. The audience will then assume that every one of your specifics could go just as deep, and they will feel a sense of the breadth and the depth of your point, even if you don't have time to detail all your evidence.

Know Your Evidence

The "many and quick" strategy can lead to abuses. A few bits of shallow knowledge can be used to deceive unsophisticated audiences. The best presenters know their subjects broadly and deeply and are prepared to offer fuller explanations. And wise listeners know that behind quick, specific evidence, a good presenter has to have deeper understanding. If listeners have any doubts about a presenter's knowledge, they must ask for more depth, or they risk being misled.

Tip 32: To Organize Points, Use the B.E.S.T. Recipe

After you have brainstormed the evidence you want to use in your talk, present your points in an organized fashion. A handy formula for organizing the points of a talk is the B.E.S.T. recipe: **Bottom line, Evidence, Summary, Transition**.

Bottom line — To open each point of your talk, state in 25 words or less the main idea of that section. Use a "signpost" like "My next point is…" or "Point #3 is…" This gives the audience a clear sense of where you are in your talk.

Motivational speaker Leo Buscaglia provides a good example of a "bottom line." To open a segment of one of his talks, he says, "Another thing we have in America is what I call 'age-ism'—we're too concerned about age. It's almost sick; in fact it is sick." He has just "bottom-lined" the point he will now support.

Evidence or examples — List the evidence, examples, statistics, stories, and analogies you have to support your point. "Signpost" this evidence with "Let me give you some examples," or "Here are some statistics you may find helpful."

Leo Buscaglia supports his point on age-ism by mentioning people he has met, listing actuarial statistics, drawing a musical analogy, and telling jokes. He names George Bernard Shaw, Goethe, Grandma Moses, Brooke Shields, and Jascha Heifetz—all in less than three minutes. His "Fast Facts" evidence is quick and convincing.

Summary of bottom line — Restate your point's main idea so the audience knows that you are emerging from specifics into a summary. Signpost your point's summary with "And so" or "To summarize this point…." (Don't say "In conclusion" unless you're at the end of your talk.)

Buscaglia ends his age-ism point with, "And so, it isn't our bodies that are essential, or our age that is essential. There's something greater than that— there's a wondrous spirit that is eternal, that we can attach no age to. Get on to that!" He has made, and clearly finished, his point.

Transition to next point — Lead the audience to your next point with a transitional statement, such as "That leads me to the next point," or "Now let's move on."

On the Axzo Press Web site is a "B.E.S.T. Recipe" form, which will help you make the points of your presentations very easy to follow.

Tip 33: Create Uplifting Conclusions

The most effective conclusions are a combination of logical and emotional elements crafted into a clear sequence. To fashion a solid, uplifting conclusion, try this recipe:

1. **Use a "stop sign."** A "stop sign" is a verbal signal that your talk is about to end—a phrase like "In conclusion" or "In summary." Say your stop sign in a clear voice, and your audience will perk up—hopefully, not because they're glad you're done, but because they know they are about to hear an important statement.

2. **Summarize your main points.** Briefly recap the main ideas you covered in your talk.

3. **Motivate the listeners.** Even in low-key presentations, an uplifting finish is often appropriate. To achieve this motivational effect, use:

   ▷ **Pronouns** — Make your talk personal. Use the words "I," "me," or "mine" to refer to your own commitment. Use the word "you"—or even better, use "we," "us," or "our" to refer to yourself and the audience as a team.

   ▷ **Optimism** — Express sincere confidence. Predict a realistic success.

   ▷ **Challenge, difficulty, effort** — Tell the audience that the ideas you have proposed may not be easy to implement. Challenge the audience to join you in moving ahead anyway.

   ▷ **The future** — Refer to times to come. Predict a brighter day as we all move forward.

   ▷ **A final uplifting phrase** — Make your very last words turn upward. Don't say "We will look to a bright future and avoid the problems of the past." Rather, say "We will avoid the problems of the past and look to a bright future." Leave the audience with a final image that is positive.

4. **Pause and say thank you.** "Thank you" signals the finish and therefore the moment listeners can react. The phrase "thank you" is, in fact, an applause cue.

5. **Pause again and solicit questions.** Make sure your pause is long enough to allow for listeners' applause or appreciative nods. Then, if appropriate, solicit and answer questions.

See the Axzo Press Web site for two documents that can help you create uplifting conclusions: "Brainstorm Uplifting Conclusions" and "Analyze Uplifting Conclusions" (a copy of the following exercise).

ANALYZE UPLIFTING CONCLUSIONS

One way to learn how to build uplifting terms into your conclusions is to analyze how professional speakers have done it for years. Following are two conclusions by very different speakers: first, the end of a speech given in 1984 by Geraldine Ferraro on the day she was selected as a candidate for the U.S. Vice-Presidency; second, the conclusion of the Inaugural Address given by President Barack Obama on January 20, 2009.

To analyze any conclusion, find the elements of challenge, optimism, future, personal pronouns, feelings, and final uplift. To help you, I've already marked and annotated these elements in Ms. Ferraro's conclusion. Use the margin to annotate your selections as you analyze President Obama's words. (See my analysis in the copy of this exercise available from the Axzo Press Web site.)

Geraldine Ferraro: "In this campaign I'm going to take our case for a better future to those Americans. I've won their support in Queens, because they know I'll fight for them, and I'm eager now to win their support throughout the nation. When Fritz Mondale asked me to be his running mate, he sent a powerful signal about the direction he wants to lead our country.

I
future
challenge, effort
I, feelings

future
we (our)

American history is about doors being opened, doors of opportunity for everyone, as long as you're willing to earn it. The last few hours, I've got to tell you, I've been on the phone, talking with friends and supporters around the country. There's an electricity in the air, an excitement, a sense of new possibilities and of pride. My good friend Charlie Rangel, congressman from Harlem, said to me "Gerry, my heart is full." So is mine. Fritz Mondale knows what America is really about, and I'm honored to join him in this campaign for the future. Thank you."

optimism,
challenge, effort

optimism
my

I, feelings

future, final uplift

Barack Obama: America, in the face of our common dangers, in this winter of our hardship, let us remember these timeless words [of George Washington, quoted earlier]. "With hope and virtue, let us brave once more the icy currents, and endure what storms may come. Let it be said by our children's children that when we were tested we refused to let this journey end, that we did not turn back nor did we falter; and with eyes fixed on the horizon and God's grace upon us, we carried forth that great gift of freedom and delivered it safely to future generations." Thank you. God bless you. And God bless the United States of America.

Tip 34: Handle Questions with Care

When you answer questions, listeners find out how much you really know about your topic. So handling questions well can be a real boost to your credibility and success as a presenter. To answer questions well, follow these guidelines:

▶ **Anticipate questions.** Before the presentation, brainstorm several tough questions you think you'll be asked. Prepare clear, well-phrased answers.

▶ **Specify when you want the Q&A session.** In your introduction, say that you welcome questions either anytime, after sections of the talk, or at the end of the talk. Questions anytime may make your talk longer, but the interactivity can make your talk more engaging.

▶ **Listen carefully to questions.** Don't complete questioners' thoughts—that can be insulting.

▶ **Always support questioners.** Never put anyone down for asking a question. Put-downs make enemies. But be aware that presenters can insult questioners unintentionally by making a comment intended as neutral. For example, suppose a presenter prefaces his response with "I thought I covered that, but I'll explain it again" or "As I said earlier…." Hear how these comments sound insulting?

▶ **Beware of saying "Good question."** If you say it to Joe, you'll have to say it to everybody, or risk making people think their questions aren't as good as Joe's.

▶ **If appropriate, repeat (or restate) the question.** Restating questions is not always necessary. But do restate questions if they are complex or unclear, or if some listeners can't hear the questions.

▶ **Break out multiple-part questions.** If you're asked a three- or four-part question, you can answer only the first part of the question and then say, "Now, what was your next question?" Handling the questions one at a time is much easier and just as effective.

▶ **Involve the entire audience in your answer.** Even though one person asked the question, you should answer to everyone, but direct a bit more eye contact to the asker than to the other listeners.

▶ **If you don't know the answer, don't bluff.** Say you don't know, promise to provide the asker with an answer, and do it ASAP. This approach demonstrates an engaging "customer service" attitude.

▶ **Answer briefly whenever possible.** The fewer words you say, the more of them will be remembered. And short answers save time. Answer concisely whenever possible, but if a longer answer is appropriate, consider the Q-BEST-Q technique discussed next.

▶ **For longer answers, use the Q-BEST-Q recipe.** Some questions require complex answers with supporting evidence. Organize longer answers so that examples and evidence support a clear "bottom line" response:

1. **Q = Question repetition, if necessary.** In restating questions, use a mixture of direct or indirect restatements. Direct restatement retains the question format: "You're asking if I favor the four-day, 40-hour work week, right? My view is…." Indirect restatement incorporates the question in the first sentence of the answer: "With regard to the four-day, 40-hour work week, my view is…."

2. **B = Bottom-line answer.** Make the bottom line short and sweet. Aim for 25 words or less.

3. **E = Evidence.** Support your answer in a concise, "Fast-Facts" fashion. To continue the example above: "Let me tell you why: the four-day week will keep our office open longer every day, which helps our customers. Employees' morale will go up because they'll have more days off. We'll make better use of our computer terminals. We'll suffer no loss in output. And we'll even reduce traffic jams in our parking lot."

4. **S = Summary of the bottom line.** Restate the bottom-line answer: "And so for these reasons, I believe that yes, we should have a four-day, 40-hour work week."

5. **T = Time awareness.** Even though your answer is complex, try to keep it under a minute.

6. **Q = Questioner satisfied?** Ask the questioner, "Have I answered your question?" If she wants more, oblige her. If she's satisfied, move on. When you check back with questioners, you can keep your first answers short, elaborating only if questioners request more detail.

To help you prepare complex answers to questions, see the Axzo Press Web site for a form titled "Preparing Complex Answers."

Tip 35: Gesture from the Audience's Point of View

One of the most subtle and sophisticated nonverbal techniques you can use when presenting is the technique of gesturing from the listeners' point of view. You can use this technique when you are talking about either time or physical space.

Gesturing Time

English reads from left to right, and English texts containing timeline graphs usually depict the past on the left and the future on the right. So in effect we could say that in our English-thinking minds, time commonly flows from left to right.

When you're presenting, you can use this left-to-right time idea to create a gesture opportunity. But you're facing the audience, so your left is the audiences' right, and vice versa. So here is what your time gestures look like to the audience:

You have to gesture *backwards* for yourself to gesture correctly for the listeners.

Gesturing Space

The same principle of gesturing "backwards" for yourself applies to space, especially geography. Suppose you're talking about trips you've taken to Oregon and Vermont. How would you gesture these locations? Think of yourself as standing up in front of a map of the USA:

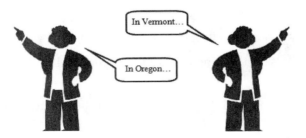

If you use time- and space-related gestures when you present, you'll add interest and energy to your delivery. And if you gesture from the audience's point of view, you'll add an extra touch of professional finesse to your presentation.

To Improve Your Gestures, Use Pantomime

In presentations, your most important visual aid is your own body language, including your gestures. But when you present, do you sometimes wonder "What should I do with my hands?" If so, you're probably not gesturing enough.

To improve your gestures, practice delivering parts of your speech in pantomime, without speaking, almost as if you were playing charades. Make your gestures imitate the missing words. Then replace your words, retaining the gestures you've practiced. The resulting increase in your presentation energy can be extraordinary.

Look for Pantomime Opportunities

Let's try to pantomime the sentence, "The success of your department is amazing." "Success" could be a thumbs-up gesture; "your department" could be two arms spreading out to the audience; "amazing" could be touching the fingertips of both hands to your temples, then flicking your hands outward. Try it! Then put the words back in and try it again. Can you sense how the gestures imitate the content?

Gesture opportunities will appear everywhere in your talk, especially from common terms. For example, you could easily gesture "you," "me," "think," "huge," "tiny," "push," "pull," "drive a car," or "divide into sections" while you speak them.

Listen for opportunities to play charades while you speak. Experiment! Use your body as well as your words to express ideas. When you use 100% of your expressive ability, the result will be a wonderfully dynamic presentation.

USE PANTOMIME TO INCREASE GESTURES

Think of gestures that express the concepts of the sentences below. Practice gesturing each sentence without words; then add the words.

1. We need to collect ideas from all three sources, throw out the bad ones, mold together the good ones, and let them grow.

2. All of the points on the flipchart are important to all of you, and especially to me.

3. So far we've been fighting each other, or at least passing each other's ideas by. We need to start working together.

Try this technique with a few sentences from a presentation you'll give soon.

Tip 36: Improve Your Voice "Music"

To play a musical instrument well, you have to play loud enough to be heard, you have to eliminate mistakes and "noise," and of course, you have to hit the notes. Did you know that to speak well, you need to do the same things with your voice?

Voice Volume: Be More than Audible

For audiences, an important measure of a speaker's confidence is his or her voice volume. Yet the single most frequent suggestion I make when I coach presenters is "Speak louder." Oh, I can usually hear them—they're audible. But probably 40% of them aren't loud enough to sound confident. They're not using "presenting voices."

Finding your presenting voice. When you present, project your voice quite a bit more than when you speak one-on-one.

A good way to find your presenting voice is to invite a colleague to a room where you might typically present. Have your colleague sit in the back of the room. Then speak for a few seconds, perhaps saying something you know well, like your name and address, in a voice that you think is slightly too loud for the room.

Ask your colleague if you were too loud. If not, try again—louder! Project! (Make sure not to speak "higher"; i.e., don't raise the pitch. Just increase the volume.) Keep trying until your colleague says you are almost too loud. You may be amazed—you'll probably think you're speaking way too loud. But trust your colleague—you sound great! That's your presenting voice.

Reducing Noise: "Um" and "Ah"

The bad news is that "um," " ah," "you know," and other non-words are the noise and static of your voice music. The good news is that you can get away with a lot more of such faults in speech than you can in music. More good news is that most speakers, even excellent ones, use some non-words—but the key is that excellent speakers don't use them very much.

Listeners usually won't hear non-words unless presenters use them more frequently than five or six times per minute. So if you keep your non-words under about five per minute you'll be OK. (One of the worst offenders I ever heard was a high-ranking official who used over 50 non-words per minute.)

How to reduce your non-words. The best way is to ask a colleague to help you practice your speech. Have him listen hard for your non-words and snap his fingers whenever you say one. This might frustrate and embarrass you, but it will help you hear them, which is the key to reducing or eliminating them.

Another way is to listen to other people talk, and count (silently!) their non-words. Or count them in the voicemail messages people leave for you. Raising your general awareness of non-words will help you get the noise out of your own voice music.

The Everyday Notes of Your Voice

Did you know that when you speak, you're actually singing? The average speaker uses more than an octave of notes in everyday speech. You may not notice this because in speech, your "notes" are not usually discrete and sustained as they would be if you were singing a song. Rather, your voice slides through its "music." This sliding is called the "intonation" (or "inflection") of your voice.

In general, the wider the range of your intonations, the better. Sometimes the only difference between a good presenter and a boring one is the range of voice intonation. In fact, the word "monotonous" comes from "mono-tone"—one note. So a key to the dynamism of your voice is the music of your intonations.

Testing your voice notes. One way to hear your voice intonations without being distracted by your words is to try a simple test: Speak with your mouth shut. Just hum your sentences. All you'll hear is intonation. For example, say, "Do you really think this will work?"—first normally, and then with your mouth shut, just humming the sentence.

What did you hear? A flat line with a little rise at the end? If so, your voice was monotonous and boring. Or did you hear a musical roller coaster of ups and downs? If so, great! You're making voice music.

The voice musicians of radio and TV. Some of the best voice musicians are media announcers. Listen to NBC's Brian Williams read the news; he's terrific. Listen to radio announcers or voice-over announcers read TV commercials. They have loud and clear voice volume, they use few if any non-words, and their intonations can be amazing. Try to ignore their words; just hear their music. Most good announcers are wonderful at making anything they say sound fascinating—which, by the way, is exactly why they were hired.

To develop your own voice music, imitate good announcers. When you're driving home or watching TV, listen to any five seconds of an announcer's voice, turn down the volume, and imitate what you heard. Try to sound exactly the same. Then turn up the volume and try again. Don't worry if your voice sounds exaggerated—remember, you're just experimenting, just playing with voice music.

The next exercise, "Use Powerful Voice Intonations," is also available on the Axzo Press Web site.

USE POWERFUL VOICE INTONATIONS

Use the statements below to practice speaking with a wide range of voice music notes. Practice speaking each one with real feeling, real conviction. Practice humming the statements, too, and listen to your intonations.

To increase the energy of your voice, try punching the air with your fist as you speak. (When you throw your body into a statement, your voice dynamism tends to increase.)

1. I told you I don't want to be a part of it! Now leave me alone!

2. This is a bargain you absolutely cannot afford to pass up! Everything— that's right, everything—is 50% off!

3. Are you kidding? You saved my life! I'll never be able to repay you!

4. We will not give up! We will fight this! And we will win!

Tip 37: To Improve Eye Contact, Think: "Who's the Sleepiest?"

Napoleon said, "To convince a man, one must speak to his eyes." Modern studies on presentation skills agree. Good eye contact is one of the most powerful ways to retain an audience's attention.

Common Eye-Contact Mistakes

We've all seen presenters neglect the quality of their eye contact, spending too much time reading their notes or looking at their visuals. Perhaps the presenters look above or below the audience, or glance at them fleetingly, looking but not seeing. Audiences interpret the presenter's poor eye contact as lack of confidence—in himself and in his own ideas. "If he's unsure," they think, "so are we—about him!"

Ask Yourself Specific Questions

The real reason you should look at listeners is to get feedback from them. You want to know how they're responding to you, so you can adjust if necessary. A way to focus on their feedback, and therefore on their faces and eyes, is to continually ask yourself a specific question, such as, "Who's the sleepiest audience member?" or "Who seems to like this talk?" or "Who needs more information?"

Practice When You're Not Presenting

Practice this eye-contact question at a meeting when you're not presenting. Look around at each person just long enough to judge how sleepy he or she is. Think about how you are looking at them, how long you dwell on each face. That's how you should be observing your audiences when you give presentations.

When you present, try to look at everybody. Don't neglect the people at the corners of the room or in that easily overlooked first row. Really observe them; try to absorb their reactions. If you observe with a specific question in mind—like "Who's the sleepiest?"—you'll communicate with the audience, not at them. Even though only you are speaking, your presentation will become a powerful dialogue.

Tip 38: For Impromptu Presentations, Answer Three Questions

An easy and effective way to give impromptu presentations is simply to ask and then answer three questions about the topic you're discussing.

How Carol Survived a Surprise Presentation

Suppose Carol's boss suddenly turns to her at a meeting and says, "Please give us a report on what the Indirect Distribution department has been up to." She doesn't panic; she says, "Well, the three most important questions to ask about indirect distribution are, 'What's the overall plan?' 'What are the major steps in the plan?' and 'When will the plan be completed?'" Next, she goes back and fills in a reasonably detailed answer to each question. She sums up with, "That's a quick look at indirect distribution."

Notice the structure of Carol's reply: she states the topic, poses all three questions, goes back to answer each one, and then restates the topic.

Carol probably could have used other questions, too ("Who are the indirect agents? What are their sales goals? How are they doing on these goals?"). And after she finishes her three questions and answers, she has the option to ask the audience, "What other questions about indirect distribution can I answer for you?"

Here's another strategy Carol could have used: When she was first asked to speak, she might have asked the listeners, "Before I describe things that may not interest you, tell me: what questions can I answer for you?" Then she could have followed the listeners' lead, letting them determine the structure of her talk.

Giving an excellent impromptu talk is no harder than answering a few questions.

Use Impromptu Techniques to Create "Press Conference" Presentations

If you give regular talks to the same group of people, experiment with a "press conference" instead of a standard presentation. The press conference presentation is very simple and similar to the impromptu strategy: List the major sections of your talk, and answer questions on each section for a set time. That's all there is to it. A press conference focuses only on what the audience wants to hear, and it's much easier to prepare than a regular talk.

Tip 39: To Sell to a V.I.P., Converse; Don't Lecture

Over the years I've coached hundreds of excellent sales professionals, many of whom were kind enough to share with me their experiences giving one-on-one sales presentations to senior executives. As I assembled their comments for this Tip, I was reminded how valuable their ideas are. So get ready for a lot of great ideas about selling to "VIP," our composite V.IP.!

Before Your Sales Meeting

Prepare! Know VIP's business; get a feel for her company's strategies. Do corporate research; know about VIP's company's stock and financial reports. Know the mission statement of VIP's company. Know VIP's competitors and the status of VIP's industry. Know what's important to VIP—her short- and long-term goals and bottom line.

Call the day before to confirm the meeting. Know your objective for the meeting; have a call plan. Adjust what you say to the exact purpose of your meeting. Know beforehand what to cut from your presentation if time runs short. Always bring value: Know your value, plan to bring value, and have a clear value statement. Plan to adjust this value statement to benefit the VIP.

Have respect for VIP's level and for the type of person VIP is. Know that you are VIP's equal as a person, but VIP is your valued client.

During the Meeting

Respect VIP's time—never, ever be late. Observe VIP's office or surroundings; get a feel for VIP's personality. Thank VIP for her time for the appointment.

Be professional. Look VIP in the eye; make good eye contact. Have good posture.

Be prepared if VIP asks: "Who are you? What value do you bring?" Have a benefit statement for the meeting; e.g., "At the end of this meeting you should have…."

Ask open-ended, leading questions. Don't ask insincere questions. Have one key question, but also a series of questions arranged in priority order in case you don't have time for them all. Questions to consider using include:

- ▶ "Were you satisfied with last year's performance?"
- ▶ "How do you measure success?"
- ▶ "What are your plans or strategies for next year?"
- ▶ "What keeps you up at night?"
- ▶ "How do you see us helping you?"

When you speak about your product or service, get quickly to the point, the "meat." Use a "hook" to pique VIP's interest. Have a brief, 25-words-or-less summary or definition ready. Be clear and concise; stay on track. Focus on your key points. Speak on a macro-level; don't be too detailed or too technical. Remember "ABC": "Always Be Closing."

Give examples of success stories; use VIP's language. Be polite and tactful. Use the term "my team" instead of "I"; mention competitors (but do not denigrate them); never "B.S." VIP, and don't make promises for someone else.

Try not to say "um" or "uh."

Conduct a conversation, not a presentation. Be aware of "talk-time distribution" (how much of the conversation is generated by each person). Aim for 50% for you and 50% for VIP—or even better, 30% for you, and 70% for VIP.

Assume nothing and be ready for anything—anticipate a wide variety of possible questions and responses from VIP. Stop talking when VIP starts talking; but even though you let VIP interrupt you, you should never interrupt VIP. Don't contradict VIP; don't say "You're wrong."

Listen carefully. Take notes, and let VIP see that you are taking notes. Ask confirming questions, or repeat back to confirm understanding, or both. Watch and read VIP's body language, and try to mirror VIP's body language and demeanor.

Ask VIP's permission to move the meeting forward through each of its steps.

As the Meeting Ends

Know when to end the meeting. Either ask about time if it is running short, or if time runs out and VIP doesn't stop the meeting, keep going. Have an action plan. Get buy-in for a next step; recap and confirm what you have agreed to.

Ask for—or position yourself for—further contact, perhaps with VIP or with other point persons or decision makers. Ask VIP who would be the point person for future contacts. Ask if you can contact VIP again, perhaps after having met other contacts.

Thank VIP at the end of the meeting; if possible, leave VIP with something tangible as a token or reminder.

Tip 40: Deliver Smooth Team Presentations

If you and a colleague are sharing the delivery of a presentation, consider the following suggestions to help you work as a competent, coordinated team.

▶ **Coordinate your setup activities.** Who will set up what? Who will greet participants who arrive early?

▶ **Perfect your opening statements.** First impressions are critical, so know what your introduction "recipe" will be. Decide if one of you will introduce both of you, or if each of you will introduce himself, or if you'll introduce each other.

▶ **Focus on continuity.**

  ❑ Work on transitions, e.g.: "Now that I've discussed (A), George will discuss (B). George?" "Thanks, Martha. Yes, let's now discuss (B)."

  ❑ Refer to each other's remarks, e.g.: "This ties back to George's point earlier…" or "As George will detail for you in a minute…."

▶ **Watch each other's presentations.** Recommended percentages of time you spend:

  ❑ Paying rapt attention to your co-presenter   65%

  ❑ Watching the listeners for cues   30%

  ❑ Checking your notes, if necessary   5% or less

  ❑ Yawning, stretching, sleeping   0%

▶ **Have a set of private signals.**

  ❑ From the offstage presenter to the onstage presenter: Have signals for "Louder," "Slower," "Talk less," and "Call on me/bring me in."

  ❑ From the onstage presenter to the offstage presenter: Have signals for "Help!" and "Next slide, please" (if necessary).

▶ **Help fix each other's mistakes.** If your co-presenter makes an important mistake (not a tiny slip-up), gently help him or her fix it right away.

▶ **Handle questions smoothly.**

  ❑ Avoid "piling on" an answer. If your co-presenter has answered a question adequately, resist adding more.

  ❑ To hand off a question to your co-presenter, use the Name-Question-Name technique: "George, Mr. Client just asked us about (A), and I know that's really your area. What do you think, George?"

Tip 41: Think of Mistakes as Assets

If you make an occasional mistake in your delivery—if you lose your place, say, or click to the wrong slide—don't worry. See the moment as an opportunity to recover like a pro. Fix the mistake with a minimum of fanfare; take your time to find your place or find the correct slide, perhaps calmly saying, "Let's try this one." Then forget it and proceed. Presto! You may have just improved, not hurt, your talk.

How so? Well, assuming the audience has even noticed your mistake, they have taken their cues from you. If you panicked, they're feeling embarrassed. But if you calmly recovered and moved on, they're now thinking something like "Good job... nothing's going to unravel this presenter. What a pro!"

Huge Mistake: A True Story

Once I was giving a presentation to a brand new client, trying to win a big-dollar account. Lots of important people were in the room. I was well into my talk— several minutes—but for some reason I couldn't get a reaction from anyone. The group seemed frozen, very nervous or upset. I thought, what's wrong? Finally a guy in the first row held up a piece of paper for me to see. It said, "Zip your pants."

I thought to myself, "Oh, no. This is bad." Then I thought, "OK, forget it. Keep going." So I fixed the problem as discreetly as I could, and said, "Gosh, I'm sorry. That's never happened to me before. Now let's see, back to point #2...." It wasn't easy, but I continued. At the end, two executives came up to me and said, "Nice recovery." One of them added, "But when you come back, check your fly, OK?" I said "You bet. No problem."

Guess what? They did bring me back. We got the account. I went in there with my zipper undone and they still hired me.

Some Advice on Mistakes and Recoveries

Even though mistakes can be assets, don't make mistakes on purpose. Do your homework, and always do the best you can. Keep in mind that audiences will not forgive avoidable errors of fact or mistakes caused by laziness.

But if you make a mistake, stay calm. Think, "This is an opportunity." Take your time and fix the mistake. Then continue, with minimal or no apology. If the mistake doesn't seem to bother you, it probably won't bother the audience.

Remember that for most audiences, professionalism outranks perfection. Think about it—if you ever saw a perfect presentation, would you like it? Maybe not. It might be too slick, too robotic. What audiences like is a solid effort by a real person who may be fallible, but who has the confidence to fix mistakes and continue.

Tip 42: When Presenting, Be Just Nervous Enough

Most presenters—even seasoned professionals—feel nervous stress before presenting. And that's a very good thing.

A *good* thing? Yes. Remember Nancy Kerrigan, the Olympic skater? She won the silver medal in figure skating at the 1994 Olympics. Once a reporter asked her why she didn't win gold. Interestingly, she said she fell short because she just wasn't nervous enough. She was too relaxed—she just went out and skated.

Stress helps star athletes and other top performers perform better. Stress creates focus, energy, and intense desire to achieve excellence. So stress can help us deliver better presentations. But we have to find the right level of stress—and for most of us, that means reducing it, not increasing it like Nancy Kerrigan should have done.

MANAGING STRESS

1. List all the stress symptoms you experience before giving presentations: clammy hands, a sense of confusion, a dry mouth, an "I'd do anything to get out of this" attitude, and so on.

    ▷ _____

    ▷ _____

    ▷ _____

    ▷ _____

    ▷ _____

2. Go back to your list and circle the two or three symptoms that are strongest or that you notice first when you feel nervous before speaking.

3. Identify these symptoms as either mainly psychological or mainly physical, and tally the results below. How many of your main symptoms are:

    Psychological: _____

    Physical: _____

4. Before we look at specific stress symptoms, let's consider general techniques for reducing presentation stress:

    a. Organized preparation — Use a repeatable, dependable process or system to organize your presentation.

    b. Progressive rehearsal — Practice your presentation a few times, in progressively more realistic circumstances; e.g., start practicing in your car, and end by doing a dry run in the actual presentation room.

CONTINUED

CONTINUED

5. Now, back to your specific symptoms. Depending on how you notice your stress, try techniques below that address either physical or psychological symptoms.

Physical Techniques	Psychological Techniques
Rib cage breathing. Breathe deeply for two minutes. Feel your rib cage expand and contract.	**Redefine stress as excitement.** Stress is what you feel when you really want to do well, even in your hobbies.
Progressive relaxation. Tense and relax your legs, torso, arms—all the way up.	**Visualize yourself succeeding.** Make a detailed mental movie of yourself giving a great talk. Play the film over and over in your mind.
Funny faces. Stretch and relax your neck and face. (You'll look strange, so do this in private.)	**"Oh boy," not "oh no."** Think of your presentation as a huge opportunity to be an Olympian superstar. Go for it!
Air raid siren. To loosen your voice, hum your highest note; then slide down slowly to your lowest note.	**Go for gold, settle for silver.** Think about "excellence," not necessarily "perfection."
The aerobic minute. Take a brisk walk just before presenting. Warm up!	**Think about the listeners' success,** not yours. They're more important than you.
Avoid caffeine and carbonation. Caffeine can make you jumpy, and carbonation can make you belch. If you're thirsty, drink warm water to relax your throat.	**Make eye contact.** Think of listeners as individuals. Make eye contact and relax.
Move around while presenting. Take a few steps; gesture; channel some of that nervous energy!	

Eight Tips for Using PowerPoint

Eight Tips for Using PowerPoint

This section gives suggestions on designing PowerPoint slides and on delivering PowerPoint slideshows—an important but sometimes neglected aspect of business presentations. You will get the most benefit out of this section if you have at least some experience putting together and delivering PowerPoint slideshows. The examples used in the section were created in PowerPoint 2007, but will work in PowerPoint 2003.

Preparing PowerPoint presentations. First, fill out the "Rumors and Findings" true/false questionnaire, available on the Axzo Press Web site. You'll find out if your opinions about preparing PowerPoint slides agree with those of the presenters I've met in my workshops and coaching sessions.

Tip 43 tells you how to save time by starting to create your presentations before opening PowerPoint.

Tips 44–46 give you ideas on how to use title designs, transition slides, and custom animation to help make your ideas crystal clear and easy to follow.

Tip 47 gives you ways to add visual enhancements to emphasize key ideas of your presentation.

Tip 48 suggests a way you can tailor a single slideshow to appeal to completely different groups, and gives you options for adding more information to your presentations "on the fly."

Delivering PowerPoint presentations. Before you look at the Tips, fill out a second "Rumors and Findings" true/false questionnaire; this one is about delivering presentations. (This questionnaire is also available on the Axzo Press Web site.) You'll see if your opinions about using slides agree with the opinions of presenters I've met.

Tip 49 recommends an awareness of audio-visual cooperation, without which presenters compete with their own slides and undermine their own presentations. This Tip also gives you suggestions on using a laser pointer and speaker's notes during presentations.

Tip 50 recommends ways to use your movements within the presentation room to help audiences understand how your talk is organized.

A Bonus Tip, available on the Axzo Press Web site, gives you a list of ideas to keep in mind when you're setting up and using laptops and projectors for your PowerPoint presentations.

Tip 43: Start Creating Your Presentations Without PowerPoint

If you start creating your presentation by opening up Microsoft PowerPoint right away, you might be doing it the hard way. If you don't have your content brainstormed before you start your slides, you'll end up trying to form ideas and make attractive slides at the same time. Mixing these two processes can throw you off track and give you writer's block.

You'll create presentations more efficiently if you plan, brainstorm, and organize the verbal part of your presentation first, without PowerPoint. The process I use is detailed in "How to Prepare a Presentation," available from the Axzo Press Web site. Here's a quick overview of the key steps:

1. Analyze your goals and listeners.

2. Brainstorm and organize your content.

3. Create a strong introduction.

4. Organize the content of your points.

5. Create a strong conclusion.

After you've roughed out your verbal presentation, start your slides. The graphic below illustrates how you can use a sticky-note organizing page (see Tip 17) to make your first two slides: the title slide and the agenda.

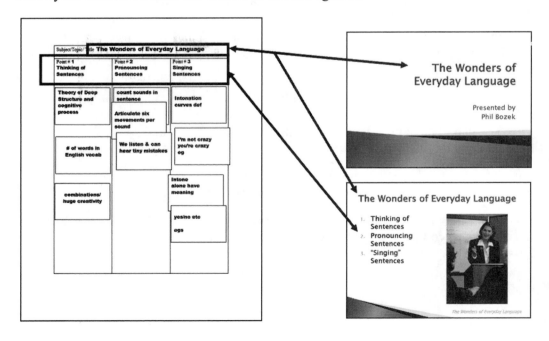

Then make the rest of your slides, adapting the same brainstorming form. The graphic below illustrates how you would take information from the form to make a slide for your first point. Notice that the language of the brainstorming is modified to make bullet points on the slide:

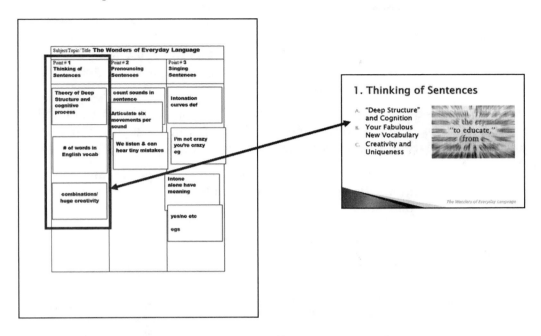

Make the rest of your slides the same way. Then make an extra copy of slide #2, your agenda (or "directory") slide, and move it to the end of your presentation. You'll use it again when you do your conclusion.

If you use brainstorming and organizing before you use PowerPoint, determining the content of your slides is easy!

Tip 44: Use Directory Visuals to Focus Your Audience

An effective way to visually organize complex information is to show two visuals at the same time: a main agenda or "directory," and a PowerPoint slide that lists bullet points like a "subdirectory" of the directory. Sometimes called the "directory-subdirectory" or "PowerPoint plus" technique, this visual style is easy to use and makes a presentation easy to follow.

This technique is especially useful for presenting information that is new, difficult, or particularly important. It's also useful for helping listeners find their place if they get distracted, have to step out for a minute, or come in late.

Let's see how the technique works. Look carefully at the presenter below, and his two visuals. What information can you gather about his talk?

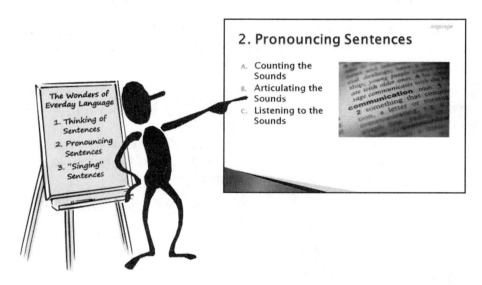

Well, the chart on the left tells you that the talk's title is "The Wonders of Everyday Language" and the talk has three parts. The slide on the right tells you that we're now in part two, "Pronouncing Sentences," and part two has three sections. Because the presenter is pointing to a specific bullet on the slide, you know he's now talking about "Articulating the Sounds."

You knew all that, without hearing any of the talk, because the presenter used the directory-subdirectory technique. In our example, the flipchart on the left is the directory; the slide on the right is a subdirectory.

When you use directory-subdirectory visuals, it's almost impossible for your audience to get lost.

Using the Directory-Subdirectory Technique

1. Choose any combination of two workable visuals. Use a flipchart or whiteboard to complement your PowerPoint slides.

2. Put your directory on the audience's left and the subdirectory on their right, because English reads left to right. (If you present in Arabic, reverse them!)

3. Leave your directory up for the whole talk, and change subdirectory slides as you move from point to point.

4. Make sure that your subdirectories' main titles exactly match the language in your directory, as in the example we saw.

5. Point to ideas on the screen as you discuss them. Use your hand or a pointer.

If Two Visuals Aren't Available, Use "Supertitles"

Flipcharts and whiteboards aren't always available, they don't work in large rooms, and, well, they're old-school. But with just PowerPoint slides and only one projector, you can still achieve clear visual organization.

One way is to use "supertitles" on your subdirectory visuals. A supertitle is the title of your whole talk, placed on every subdirectory slide. For example, suppose you're giving the "Wonders of Everyday Language" presentation:

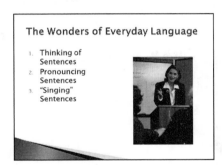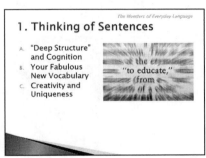

This example shows two slides: the directory slide on the left and a subdirectory slide on the right.

The subdirectory has the supertitle, "The Wonders of Everyday Language," in small letters in the top-right corner. (You can also put it in the bottom-right corner, but most presenters I've met prefer the top-right.) Supertitles constantly remind the audience of your presentation's main title.

Note: You don't need a supertitle on your directory slide because the main title is already there, in big letters.

If you use directory-subdirectory visuals, your listeners will always know exactly where you are. You'll present more clearly, even if your information is complex, listeners get distracted, or listeners come in late.

Tip 45: Use "Signpost" Slides

If you're a good presenter, you probably use verbal "signposts" like "Today we'll cover A, B, and C" and "Let's move to the next point." Signposts help listeners stay on track. If you add "transition slides" to verbal signposts, you can also help listeners remember the context of your points and the main idea of your talk.

Do good listeners forget main ideas? Yes, sometimes they do. A listener might be paying attention, watching you make a point on a slide, and suddenly think: "Yes, I get this slide, but what was the main idea again?" He may actually have forgotten.

1. Using Transition Slides as Signposts

One way you can help is to use directory-subdirectory visuals (see Tip 44). Another way is to reuse directory slides when you move from one point to another, giving the audience a transitional "glance at the map" before you proceed.

In the "Progressive Bolding" presentation (available on the Axzo Press Web site), you'll find an example of what a directory slide might look (and sound) like. View the presentation in Slide Show view in PowerPoint. As the presentation moves from slide 9 to slide 10, here's what transition slides will look (and sound) like:

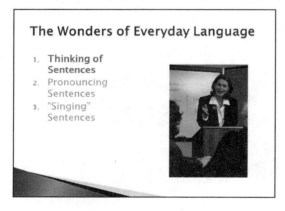

Slide 10:
"Now that we've discussed 'Thinking of Sentences,'…"

[Click to advance to the next slide]

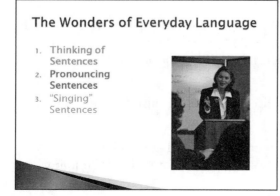

Slide 11:
"…let's move on to **[point to slide]** 'Pronouncing Sentences.'"

[Click to advance to the next slide]

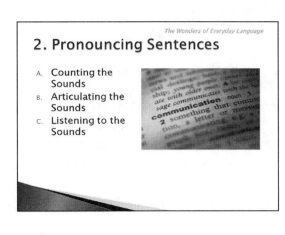

Slide 12:
"Now, 'Pronouncing Sentences' consists of…"

[Point to A, B, and C while listing them out loud.]

As you see, instead of moving from one point straight to the next, the presenter provides visual signposts by redisplaying her directory slide. She can also gesture to the slides and use verbal signposts like "OK, let's move on."

If aspects of your presentation are long or complex, use this technique with subdirectory slides as well. You can do this by repeating subdirectory slides between detailed content slides and by adding custom animation.

Use all of your resources—transition slides, gestures, and verbal cues—to help your audience follow your presentation.

2. Using Slide Sequences as Signposts

Another way to help your listeners stay on track is to design slide sequences instead of just slides. A slide sequence is a series of nearly identical slides with highlighted features that change as your slides advance, showing the audience exactly which point you are discussing.

Slide sequences look like custom animations built into one slide, but they're actually just successive slides. Slide sequences use more slides and memory than animations do, but for many presenters, slide sequences are easier to create and use.

Two of my favorite ways to create slide sequences involved what I call "progressive bolding" and "arrow advance."

"Progressive Bolding" Slide Sequences

To create a progressive bolding sequence on a slide with three discussion points on it, perform the following steps:

1. Copy the slide and paste it twice.

2. On the first slide, emphasize the first point and de-emphasize the other points with formatting:

    ▷ **Emphasized point** — Apply Bold and change the font color to something that will stand out and look good on the slide (I used a bright blue).

    ▷ **De-emphasized points** — Change the font color to a lighter color (I used a light gray).

3. On the second slide, use the methods in step 2 to emphasize the second point and de-emphasize the first and third points.

4. On the third slide, use the methods in step 2 to emphasize the third point and de-emphasize the first and second points.

Using the steps just described, here's what a "progressive bolding" slide sequence would look and sound like (display the presentation in Slide Show view and move from slide 11 to slide 12):

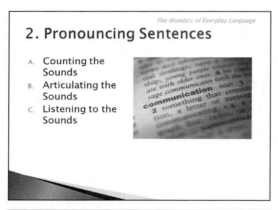

As slide 12 appears:
"In 'Pronouncing Sentences,' I'll cover A, B, and C."

[Point to A, B, and C while listing them out loud. Click to advance to the next slide.]

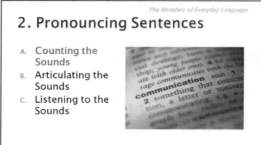

Slide 13:
"Let's start with A…"

[Explain details. Then click to advance to the next slide.]

Slide 14:

"Let's move to B…"

[Explain details. Click to advance to the next slide.]

Slide 15:

"OK, on to C…"

[Explain details. Click to advance to the next slide.]

Slide 16:

"So, in 'Pronouncing Sentences,' we've covered A, B, and C."

[Point to A, B, and C while listing them out loud.]

A note on timing: The first and last slides in our example (slides 12 and 16) are transition slides, in view for only two or three seconds each. The speaker's comments on these slides are very brief. Only slides 13–15 are shown and explained at length.

The "Arrow Advance" Technique

The "Arrow advance" presentation uses a little marker arrow (I use a bright red one) to achieve the same tracking effect as progressive bolding. You can create your own custom arrow by doing the following:

▶ **In PowerPoint 2003** — On the Drawing toolbar, display the AutoShapes list and select a Block Arrow. Then draw the arrow on the slide.

▶ **In PowerPoint 2007** — On the Insert tab, display the Shapes list and select a Block Arrow. Then draw the arrow on the slide.

After you've created the first arrow, perform the following steps:

1. Resize the arrow, color it, and place it in the desired location.

2. Copy the arrow and paste it twice. (We are using the sample slides in the following dialogue as a guide.)

3. Place one arrow to the left of each numbered point. (Make sure the arrows line up vertically with each other. If you don't line them up, it will look like the arrows shift to the right or left when you transition from one slide to the next.)

4. Copy the slide and paste it twice.

5. On the first slide, delete the arrow next to the second and third points.

6. On the second slide, delete the arrow next to the first and third points.

7. On the third slide, delete the arrow next to the first and second points.

Those are the steps I used to create the following demo presentation, where the arrow shapes lead into and out of point #2. (Open the "Arrow Advance" presentation, available on the Axzo Press Web site.)

As slide 10 appears, the presenter might say:

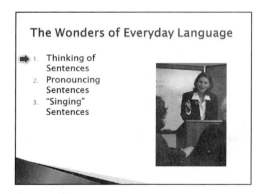

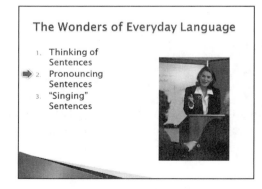

Slide 10: "Now that we've covered 'Thinking of Sentences...'"

[Click to advance to the next slide.]

Slide 11: "...let's move on to 'Pronouncing Sentences.'"

[Click to advance to the next slide.]

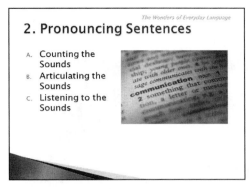

Slide 12: "In 'Pronouncing Sentences,' I'll cover A, B, and C."

[Click to advance to the next slide.]

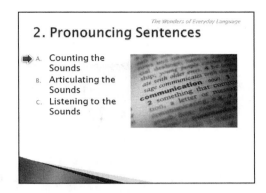

Slide 13: "Let's start with A…"

[Explain details. Click to advance to the next slide.]

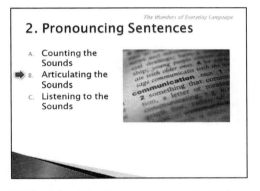

Slide 14: "Let's move on to B. This means…"

[Explain details. Click to advance to the next slide.]

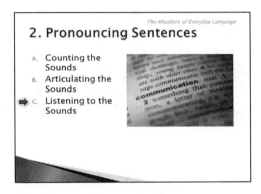

Slide 15: "OK, on to C…"

[Explain details. Click to advance to the next slide.]

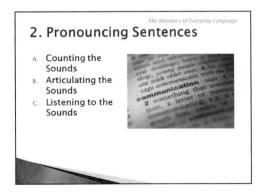

Slide 16: "So, in 'Pronouncing Sentences,' we covered…"

[Click to advance to the next slide.]

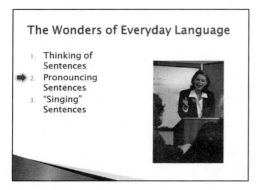

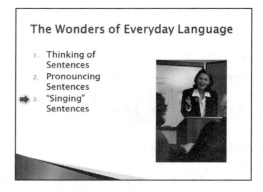

Slide 17: "Let's move from 'Pronouncing Sentences'…"

[Click to advance to the next slide.]

Slide 18: "…to 'Singing Sentences.'"

[Click to end the presentation.]

Like the progressive bolding technique, the "arrow advance" method creates a progressive sequence that is easy for the audience to follow.

Custom animation: *If you're feeling adventurous, try the progressive bolding and arrow advance techniques by using PowerPoint's custom animation feature. Examples of the demo presentations with custom animation effects are available on the Axzo Press Web site.*

Tip 46: Use Dynamic On-Screen Menus

Dynamic on-screen menus give your presentation's slides a clear, organized look. Your complete agenda ("directory") is always visible, and it has progressive highlighting to show everyone exactly where you are in your presentation.

Just Like Web Pages and Cable News

Web pages use menus to let you select where you want to go. And cable news shows like those on CNN and ESPN use similar on-screen "menus" to show you what they're talking about now and what's coming up soon.

One thing that CNN and ESPN do not do, however, is show the items they've already covered. They have no need to. But our menu model does show what has been covered, because review and memory are important in business presentations.

What to Notice in These Demo Slides

The demo that follows (open the "Dynamic On-screen Menu" presentation, available on the Axzo Press Web site) shows what a sequence of slides would look like with a menu layout. I have used a "box-emphasis" technique, just to make sure you can see it on these pages, but progressive bolding or arrow-advance (see Tip 45) would also look good. Also, as in Tip 45, I have used slide sequences instead of custom animation to achieve these special effects.

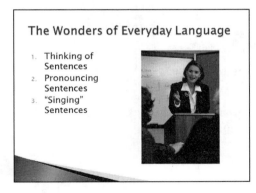

Slide 2: (Title slide) "Good morning."

[Greet the audience, name the topic, give credentials, and give benefits. (See introduction recipe, Tip 30.) Click to slide 3.]

Slide 3: "Today I'll cover…"

[Read through the numbered list; give Q&A rules. (See introduction recipe, Tip 30). Click to slide 4.]

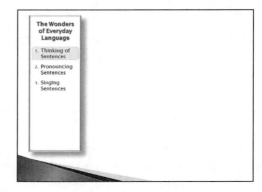

Slide 4: "I'll move our agenda off to the left so we can keep it in view during our discussion."

[Click to slide 5. Menu box appears around point #1.]

Slide 5: "Let's get started with point #1."

[Click to slide 6. Slide content fades in.]

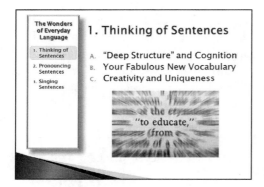

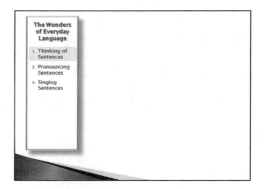

Slide 6: "I'll cover A, B, and C."

[Explain details. Click to slide 7. Slide content disappears.]

Slide 7: "Now we've finished Point 1, so…"

[Click to slide 8. Menu box moves to point #2.]

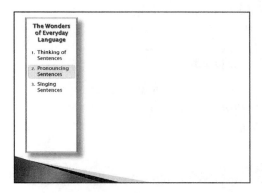

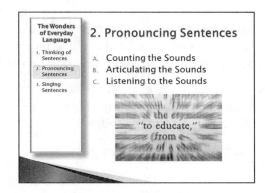

Slide 8: "…let's move to point #2, 'Pronouncing Sentences.'"

[Click to slide 9. Slide content fades in.]

Slide 9: "Under 'Pronouncing Sentences,' I'll cover A, B, and C."

[Explain details. Click to slide 10. Slide content disappears.]

Slide 10: "We've finished point 2…"

[Click to slide 11. Menu box moves to point #3.]

Slide 11: "…so let me explain what I mean by the phrase 'Singing Sentences.'"

[Click to end the slide show.]

A note on the size of on-screen menus. One issue with any on-screen menu is how much of the screen it should occupy. It has to be big enough to be seen without dominating the screen and thereby confusing the audience. You can use the "Dynamic On-Screen Menu" presentation, provided on the Axzo Press Web site, to create your own presentation, but you might need to adjust the menu's size.

As you look at the example provided, you'll notice that the menu layout uses a custom master page. To understand the menu layout, display Slide Master view and observe the last slide in the list. As you do so, you'll see:

▶ **In PowerPoint 2007:**

❑ The slide master was created by copying the Title, Text and Content Layout and modifying its elements.

❑ Point to the slide master icon (in the left pane) to display the tooltip. It's named "Wonders of Everyday Language" and is applied to slides 4 and 5.

❑ The menu box is formatted with options on the Drawing Tools | Format tab, and the box is behind the text (it was sent to the back of the Arrange order).

❑ "The Wonders of Everyday Language" is in its own text box and formatted with options on the Drawing Tools | Format tab.

❑ The numbered list uses the Body style with some customization.

▶ **In PowerPoint 2003:**

❑ The slide master was created by copying the "Title, Text and Content Layout" and modifying its elements.

❑ Point to the slide master icon (in the left pane) to display the tooltip. It is named "13_Concourse Slide Master" and is applied to slides 4 and 5.

❑ The menu box was formatted with options available in PowerPoint 2003, and the box is behind the text.

❑ "The Wonders of Everyday Language" is in its own text box and formatted with options available in PowerPoint 2003.

❑ The numbered list worked well in PowerPoint 2007 but didn't translate well to PowerPoint 2003, so it has been deleted.

Custom animation: *If you're feeling adventurous, try the dynamic on-screen menu technique by using PowerPoint's custom animation feature. An example of the demo presentations with custom animation effects is available on the Axzo Press Web site.*

Tip 47: To Focus Within Complex Slides, Use On-Screen Enhancements

Ideally, PowerPoint slides should be easy to read quickly, but sometimes they can't be. If you need to show a complex slide, use on-screen enhancements to focus listeners' attention to the parts of the slide you want to discuss in detail. This technique is useful if you plan to detail only one part of a complex chart or if you want to detail parts of a complex chart in sequence. The technique is also useful if you're explaining how to use a procedure or a multi-step form.

To discuss a complex visual, you don't have to rely on pointing with your hands or a pointer. Free up your hands and use on-screen enhancements.

The enhancements you use can be either planned or spontaneous.

Planned Enhancements

Planned enhancements are ones you know for sure you're going to use, so you build them in as you design your slideshow. They consist of various highlighting devices like colored circles or boxes that you bring in over key areas of your slides. You would first show your chart without enhancements, and then use custom animation to display an enhancement like the one shown:

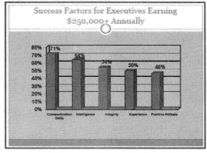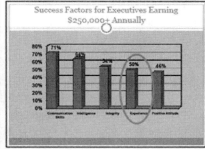

A slide in Slide Show view with an animated oval around the fourth column

To make the enhancement element above, do the following:

▶ **In PowerPoint 2003:**

1. On the Drawing toolbar, select the Oval and draw the shape on the slide.

2. Remove the Fill (if necessary). Then change the Line Style, Line Dash, and Line Color.

3. Position the oval in the correct location.

4. To make the oval appear on the screen in Slide Show view, use the slide sequence method (Tip # 45) or apply custom animation.

▶ **In PowerPoint 2007:**

1. On the Insert tab, select the Oval and draw the shape on the slide.

2. Remove the Fill (if necessary). Then, change the Line Style, Line Dash, and Line Color.

3. Position the oval in the correct location.

4. To make the oval appear on the screen in Slide Show view, use the slide sequence method (Tip # 45) or apply custom animation.

Spontaneous Enhancements

On a moment's notice, you can use PowerPoint's "marking pen" feature to make circles, draw arrows, underline words, or make other marks on slides:

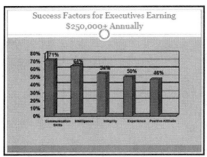 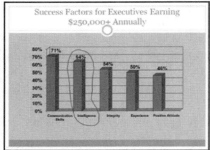

A slide in Slide Show view, with the presenter using the marking pen feature

Here's how to use this feature:

1. In Slide Show view, right-click and choose Pointer Options. (You must be in Slide Show view to see the Pointer Options command.)

2. Select a pen option.

3. Hold the mouse button down as you write or draw on your slides. Use the Pointer Options command to choose a different color ink for the markup.

   Note: If you don't want to disrupt the continuity of your presentation by right-clicking and navigating through menus, press CTRL+P to switch to using the pen, and CTRL+U to revert to the automatic pointer. Your markings are erased automatically when you move to the next slide.

Hardware for Drawing Spontaneous Enhancements

If you think you'll have difficulty using the mouse to draw shapes on slides, get an i-Pen Presentation Digital Pen/Optical Mouse Pen. With it you can easily draw shapes and even write words. In fact, the pen will even convert your handwriting into text—a big advantage for anyone with sloppy handwriting, like yours truly!

Tip 48: "Unhide" Slides if Listeners Need More Information

The situation: Suppose you have to prepare a budget presentation to give to the accountants on Tuesday morning. They'll want tons of details. But you have to give the same presentation to senior managers Tuesday afternoon, and they'll want an overview.

The problem: How can you satisfy both groups without creating two separate sets of slides? And if you're giving just an overview, how can you keep your slides simple if your listeners might ask to see deeper, more detailed information?

The solution: Prepare one set of slides. But for each point of the presentation, prepare a simple slide, and then prepare a complex slide for the same point. Repeat this alternating sequence all the way through the slideshow. Then use PowerPoint's Hide/Unhide Slides feature to show each audience only the necessary slides.

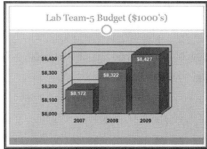 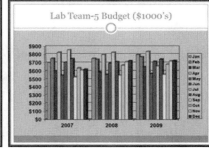

Same content on two slides: one with an overview and another with details.

In the previous example, the presentation for the Overview group uses the simple chart slide, and the complex chart slide is hidden. The same presentation will be delivered for the Details group, with the complex chart slide visible and the simple chart slide hidden.

Hiding and Unhiding Slides

To hide a slide in both PowerPoint 2003 and PowerPoint 2007:

1. On the Slides tab in Normal view, select the slide you want to hide.

2. Right-click the slide and choose Hide Slide. The hidden-slide icon appears with the slide number inside it.

   Note: The slide remains in your file, even though it is hidden when you run the presentation.

To unhide a slide:

1. On the Slides tab in Normal view, right-click the hidden slide to display the shortcut menu. Notice that the Hide Slide command is toggled on.

2. Choose Hide Slide to toggle the command off. The slide is unhidden.

Use Hyperlinks to Add Extensive Information

Hyperlinks can also help you use the same presentation for different audiences, e.g., the Overview group and the Details group. The advantage of using hyperlinks is that you can link to slides in your presentation that are not in the normal sequenced order or link to another slideshow altogether.

To use hyperlinks, you create an overview presentation with a link to the slides (in the same or another presentation) that have more details. When you present to the Details group, you use the links; and when you present to the Overview group, you don't use the links. However, if the Overview group asks for more details, you are ready with easy access to the additional information as needed.

To create a hyperlink to a custom show or location in the current presentation:

1. Select the text or object that you want to represent the hyperlink.

2. Open the Insert Hyperlink dialog box:

   ▷ **In PowerPoint 2003:** Choose Insert, Hyperlink.

   ▷ **In PowerPoint 2007:** Display the Insert tab and click the Hyperlink button.

3. Under Link to, click Place in This Document.

4. Do one of the following.

   ▷ **To link to a custom show:** In the list, select the custom show you want to go to. Check "Show and return."

   Note: A "custom show" is a presentation within a presentation. It is a way to group slides in a presentation so that you can show that section of the presentation to a particular audience

   ▷ **To link to a location in the current presentation:** In the list, select the slide you want to go to.

5. Click OK.

The Result: Tailored Presentations

A little planning, and a little design work with Hide/Unhide and hyperlinks, can make your presentations flexible and custom-fit to your listeners' needs.

Tip 49: Create Audio-Visual Cooperation

If you've invested in a new car, you should know how to drive it, right? It's the same with PowerPoint. If you've designed a great slideshow, you should know how to use it. With both cars and PowerPoint, if you can't drive, you won't get far.

One big mistake presenters make is called "audio-visual conflict"—saying one thing while displaying something else. Presenters who make this mistake inadvertently compete with their own slides and may irritate, confuse, or lose their listeners.

To fix this mistake, practice "audio-visual cooperation"—having your words and visuals in sync so that the same information that enters your listeners' ears also enters their eyes. The following techniques will help your words and your PowerPoint slides cooperate:

1. **If you need to give a lead-in statement for a slide, delay the slide.** Use the "B" button to "black" the screen, or keep the previous slide up until you finish your lead-in.

2. **Display the visual only at the exact moment you start talking about it.** When you put up a visual, your audience will look at it immediately. If you spend five seconds talking about something else before you go to the visual the audience already sees, you're competing with your visual for five seconds.

3. **Speak what's on the visual. If the slide contains words, speak the exact words of the slide.** Don't paraphrase. If the slide says "Ethics in the Workplace," don't say "Let's talk about the best way to act on the job." Rather, say "Let's discuss ethics in the workplace."

4. **Keep the audience with you.** Audiences like to absorb visuals. If a visual contains words, people often want to read all the words before they want to hear any details from the presenter. To keep listeners with you as you show visuals, choose one of these techniques:

   ▶ Read aloud through the entire visual, if it is not too wordy. Then go back and elaborate on it.

   ▶ Display the visual, be silent for a few seconds while the audience absorbs it, and then begin your discussion.

   ▶ Use PowerPoint's custom animation feature to add effects that reveal your bullet points one by one. This method reveals the information a little at a time, allowing you to comment on each bullet point without the audience reading ahead of you.

5. **Make sure that what they're seeing is what you're discussing.** When you're done with a slide, move on to the next one. If you want to talk for a while without slides, press the "B" button to "black" the screen; then press "B" again to bring the slides back into view.

Consider Your PowerPoint Delivery Technique

Here are a few other techniques that will enhance audio-visual cooperation when you're using PowerPoint:

▶ **If possible, use your hand to point to the screen.** Gestures loosen you up and help you project energy. However, if what you're pointing to is tiny, use a traditional pointer or a laser pointer. And if you're far from the screen, definitely use a laser pointer.

▶ **When using a laser pointer:**

❑ If the screen is on your left, hold the laser pointer in your left hand so you don't turn your back to the audience. If the screen is on your right, use your right hand.

❑ Extend your arm when you point. Make the laser pointer beam an obvious extension of your arm gesture.

❑ Hold the beam as steady as possible, so it doesn't jiggle on the screen.

❑ Circle objects on the screen very slowly.

▶ **Make frequent eye contact with the audience.** Make sure you're looking at your listeners more than you look at your slides.

▶ **Consider using speaker's notes.** If you use your projected slides as speaker's notes, you may turn your back on the listeners too much. Instead, use PowerPoint's notes feature or the BEST method (see Tip 32).

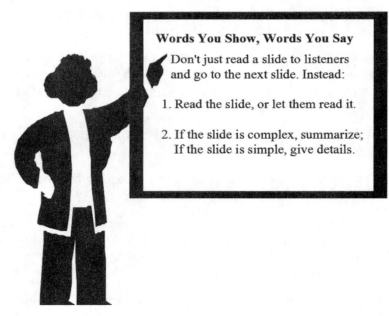

Words You Show, Words You Say

Don't just read a slide to listeners and go to the next slide. Instead:

1. Read the slide, or let them read it.

2. If the slide is complex, summarize; If the slide is simple, give details.

Tip 50: Use the Room to Clarify the Structure of Your Presentation

When audiences listen to presentations, they get structural cues from visual aids and the presenter's signpost statements. But your movements through the room can provide another valuable structural cue for your audience.

If you match your movements to topic or subtopic shifts in your talk—using a technique I call "functional movement"—your audience can get a sense of an organized flow through a defined structure.

Suppose you're giving a talk in a room with the layout shown below. You're following the introduction recipe in Tip 30, so you say and do the following things: (A) say hello and identify yourself; (B) name the topic of your talk and point to a title slide; (C) summarize your credentials in the topic; (D) explain the benefits the audience will gain from listening; and (E) preview the main points of your talk while pointing to them on the second slide (your agenda or "directory").

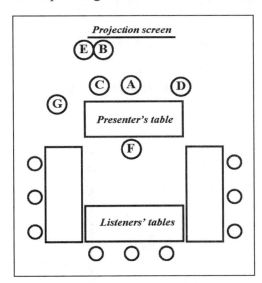

Start by doing part (A) from location "A" on the map; then move in turn to the other locations, with each movement coordinating with progress through the introduction recipe. You end at "E," near the screen again, where you forecast your points. You will have reinforced shifts in the talk's structure with your movements in the room.

You can use other kinds of functional movement throughout your presentation. A few ideas:

▶ When you want the listeners to interact with you or with each other, sit on a table or chair, or maybe even among the listeners.

▶ If you want to make your conclusion personal, come closer to the listeners, perhaps delivering your last statements from position "F."

▶ When you want to involve the listeners, or when you're telling a story, consider walking around behind the audience (or through the audience if you're in a big room).

Functional Movements and PowerPoint Slides

You can even use functional movement when displaying a bullet-point slide. Suppose you are giving your presentation in the room shown previously, and you are just about to display an important slide. How can you use your movements and gestures to make yourself most clear?

Try this movement sequence:

1. Display the new slide.

2. Immediately move to position "E" near the screen. Then, do one of the following:

    ▷ Point to the slide while reading it aloud: "Now, program development listeners consist of decision makers, advisors, users, administrators, champions, and externals." As you speak, you gesture to each term, perfectly in sync with your words.

    ▷ Ask listeners to read the slide silently. Remain silent for a few seconds while they read.

    ▷ Use a custom animation sequence, if your slide has one.

3. Point to and name the bullet point you will detail. With the first bullet point on this slide, say something like "Let's discuss decision makers in more detail."

4. Move a few steps to position "G" as you detail the bullet point. Make eye contact with your listeners!

5. To signal a shift to the next bullet point, move back to position "E" at the screen.

6. For each bullet point on the slide, repeat steps 2–5.

7. After you've detailed the last bullet point:

    ▷ Move back to position "E" near the screen.

    ▷ Gesture toward the whole slide.

    ▷ Briefly restate the main idea of the point. In this example, say something like "So that's what we mean by program development listeners."

8. For each slide with bullet points, repeat steps 1–7.

Experiment with different movements, but try not to move pointlessly. If you key your movements to your talk's structure, you'll increase your own dynamic movement while you help listeners sense the organization of your talk.

A P P E N D I X

Appendix to Part 2

Comments & Suggested Responses

Business Writing: Fact or Myth

1. Myth. See #2.

2. Fact.

3. Myth. Readers often want only what they need.

4. Myth. Many writers work more efficiently if they write quickly and imperfectly at first, using brainstorming or "Aerobic Writing" (see Tip 19). Then they perfect the document later, during revising.

5. Myth. Most readers prefer short, simple words.

6. Fact. Long, multi-subject e-mail messages are hard to label, hard to read, and hard to archive.

7. Fact. Even short, informal e-mail messages should be revised quickly. You never know where they'll be forwarded or stored.

8. Myth. This could lead to an exponential proliferation of e-mail messages. Instead, limit recipients by choosing them wisely.

9. Myth. Different people have different "reading personalities." Some readers are usually attentive and meticulous, but many are too busy, so they skim and scan for main ideas. Some people skim and scan all the time, and then sometimes go back and read carefully.

10. Myth. Personal pronouns clarify who does what and make writing friendlier.

11. Myth. Spreading out information can make it easier to read.

12. Fact. This isn't plagiarism, it's best practices.

Asking the "Big Question"

Suggested revisions.

1. "We're forming a policy that will include everyone." (8 words)

2. "If you know anyone who fits the job, let us know." (11 words)

3. "Please send me the project info ASAP. I'll have a close look. Then let's discuss it." (15 words)

50-Minute™ Series

If you enjoyed this book, we have great news for you.
There are more than 200 books available in the
Crisp Fifty-Minute™ Series.

Subject Areas Include:

Management and Leadership
Human Resources
Communication Skills
Personal Development
Sales and Marketing
Accounting and Finance
Coaching and Mentoring
Customer Service/Quality
Small Business and Entrepreneurship
Writing and Editing

For more information visit us online at

www.CrispSeries.com